Walking the Coastline
of Shetland

No. 7

Eastside

Walking the Coastline of Shetland

No. 7

Eastside

Peter Guy

The coastline of Eastside of Shetland Mainland,
and the islands of
Bressay
Noss
Whalsay
Out Skerries

The Shetland Times Ltd.,
Lerwick, Shetland.
2004

First published by The Shetland Times Ltd., 2004

ISBN 1 904746 01 2

Text © Peter Guy, 2004

Photographs © Peter Guy except where otherwise acknowledged.

A CIP catalogue record for this book is available from the British Library.

Books in the same series

No. 1 The Island of Yell
No. 2 The Island of Unst
No. 3 The Island of Fetlar
No. 4 Northmavine
No. 5 Westside
No. 6 South Mainland

Cover Photographs:

Front cover – Lighthouse on broch site, Infield, Mossbank © Peter Guy
Inserts: Sandwick, Vidlin © Bobby Tulloch
Mill Burn waterfall, Swinning Voe, Collafirth Ness © Peter Guy
Back cover: Gun gantry, Score Hill, Aith Ness, Bressay © Peter Guy

Printed and published by
The Shetland Times Ltd., Gremista, Lerwick,
Shetland ZE1 0PX, Scotland.

For Catherine

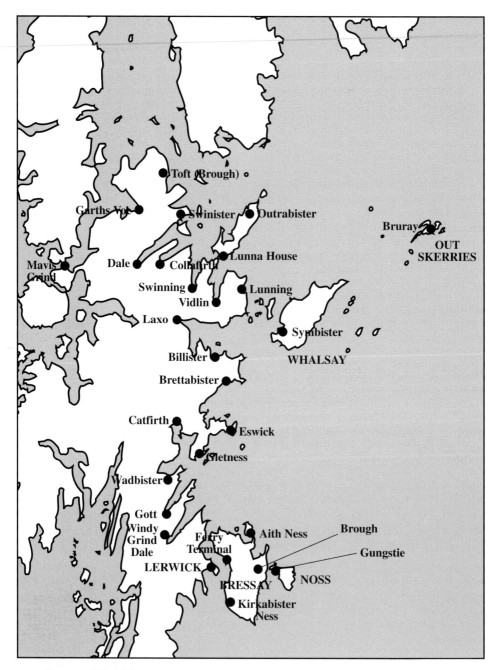

Start and finishing points of the Eastside Way, East Mainland of Shetland, Bressay, Noss, Whalsay and Out Skerries and circular walks.

EASTSIDE MAINLAND
(Whalsay, Bressay, Out Skerries and Noss)

(130 Miles / 210 Kilometers)

The Eastside Way stretches from Lerwick to Mavis Grind where it links up with the start of both the Westside Way and the Northmavine Trek. It provides a fascinating variety of experiences for the walker who may find it initially quite sheltered as he or she walks north from the busy centre of Lerwick. The island of Bressay protects both Lerwick and its harbour to a certain extent and there are a number of protected voes all the way up the coast. However, on a windy day walking, for example, on Skaw Taing on Whalsay or Ward of Outrabister on Lunna Ness, can test the hardiest walker and appropriate clothing must be worn.

There is a great diversity in the scenery which ranges from the bleak beauty of Collafirth Hill to the joyful intimacy of the Isles of Gletness. Some areas are now uninhabited whilst others, like Mossbank, have modern housing developments largely built to meet accommodation requirements of those working at Sullom Voe. The terminal itself displays the flares which signify the current exploitation of oil resources offshore.

The Eastside also possesses historic sites to match other parts of Shetland: there are at least three prehistoric standing stones, a range of broch ruins, Bronze Age burnt mounds and evidence of Norse farmhouses.

Seals are likely to accompany you as you walk the shores and whales may possibly be seen. Otters, elusive as ever, are often encountered on Lunna Ness and around North and South Nesting particularly. No bird-watcher will want to visit Shetland and not visit Noss. On the high east facing cliffs of this island Shetland's first gannet colony was established in 1911 and now boasts an estimated 5,500 nests. Thousands of other seabirds also nest here on the ledges created in the sandstone cliffs. They can, also, be viewed from a boat which makes daily excursions from Lerwick in the summer. Various other birds will be spotted on the way: you never know what to expect and king eider, for example, have been recorded in Sullom Voe.

If I had been planning this series of walking books from the start, the Eastside Way would have been number one. Lerwick provides everything a walker requires of a good base on arrival in a possibly unknown country and there is logic in discovering the town before stepping out to explore the rest of Shetland. However, the series "just growed" and it has given me enormous pleasure to walk and write about a place I love. The book, as well as describing the Eastside Way, also includes circular walks which can be walked independently of any support if a combination of car and cycle is utilised as I do, or you may wish to incorporate the use of a taxi or bus.

The islands of Whalsay, Noss, Bressay and Out Skerries are included in this book because they will be in view for much of the Eastside Way and offer more great experiences to the intrepid tramper.

Good walking!

Peter Guy
Overby
Burravoe
Yell

WALKING THE COASTLINE OF SHETLAND NO. 7

EASTSIDE MAINLAND

130 Miles (210 Kilometres)

WHALSAY, BRESSAY, OUT SKERRIES AND NOSS – EAST MAINLAND CIRCULAR WALKS

SAFETY AND CONSERVATION

Be Prepared

Have a knowledge of basic First Aid.

Know how to navigate properly using map and compass.

Carry the OS map (maps) appropriate to the walk being undertaken.

Select the right equipment for walking. Carry waterproofs, spare sweater, whistle, food, torch, gloves and balaclava.

Leave word of your planned walk and report your return.

Respect the land

Access: The Land Reform (Scotland) Act 2003 clearly sets down in statute a presumption in favour of access. The Act may come fully into force in 2004 if the Scottish Outdoor Access Code has been approved by the Scottish Parliament and local authorities begin to take up new powers. Walkers are reminded that this is an extremely sensitive issue in some parts of Scotland and we should remain mindful of the needs of those who work the land.

Take care not to drop litter. It is unsightly and can be dangerous to animals.

Remember to use gates or stiles where possible instead of climbing fences and walls.

Park with consideration, remembering that agricultural vehicles may need access near where you leave a car.

Keep dogs under full control. Remember, crofters are entitled to shoot dogs found worrying sheep.

Cliffs can present the greatest hazard and when geos (creeks) bite deep into the cliffs, the drop may be out of sight until the last moment. Keep "well in" and wear boots that give some traction on grassy slopes.

Be weatherwise

Exercise caution in low cloud or mist.

On cliffs windy and misty conditions can create dangerous situations.

Aim to complete a walk in daylight hours.

MAPS

Ordnance Survey (OS) maps are essential aids to safe walking in Eastside, as elsewhere. There are two suitable scales of map available:

Landranger series   1:50,000   1¼ in to 1 mile   2cm to 1km

Sheet 2	Shetland	Whalsay
Sheet 3	Shetland	North Mainland
Sheet 4	Shetland	South Mainland

For greater detail use **Explorer series**   1:25,000   2½ in to 1 mile   4cm to 1km

466	Shetland	Mainland South (For South Bressay)
467	Shetland	Mainland Central
468	Shetland	Mainland North East, Whalsay and Out Skerries
469	Shetland	Mainland North West, North Roe and Sullom Voe

WALKING THE LANDSCAPE AND
SEASCAPES OF SHETLAND

In the areas of Shetland, covered by this book, will be found various vibrant and caring communities, with families who have survived all the challenges and rigours of living in remote locations. Present prosperity does not mask the fact that life could often be hard in the past. We shall find the remains of many prehistoric settlement sites, often with associated cairns and burnt mounds and the means of defence using forts, duns and brochs.

There are striking standing stones, carved stones with ogham script, monastic and chapel sites. Combine these attractions with magnificent coastland scenery, stupendous bird and wildlife and a walker has a wonderful opportunity to appreciate one of the finest areas of the country. Stark the landscape may sometimes be, but people have always wanted to get here and stay and they came by sea.

The impact of the sea, both on the landscape and the inhabitants of Shetland, is always manifest. The earliest people must have made their way by some form of boat and once here, the sea was to be a better highway than any form of inland track. It is not known what boats the broch building Picts used, but the Celtic church missionary fathers ('Papa') spread from Ireland all over the north British coast and the northern islands (including Faroe) travelling in craft made from entirely perishable materials. Coracles were a Welsh specialty, for river and estuary use, but the Irish built curraghs made of ox hides stretched over a wooden frame and sealed with wool grease. Sails were useful, particularly on the 40ft long and 8ft wide vessels such as that used by St Brendan, the Navigator (490-570 AD) whose travels took him across the Atlantic and up to Shetland. Monastic cells can be found all over Shetland, some of them on sites only accessible by boat.

The book includes two places associated with the Papa, Papil Geo on Noss and possibly, on the cliff edge nearly opposite the Stack of Stoura Clett on Bressay's south east coast.

Sadly, no manuscripts survive in Shetland from the Celtic period, but one can see the glory of contemporary manuscripts in Ireland in the Book of Kells in Trinity College, Dublin, library. Neither the monks, nor anybody else, were prepared for the onslaught of the Vikings – pagan warriors who worshipped war-like Gods and who had no compunction in killing the monks and looting the monasteries. The Viking ships, dreki or dragon ships, could arrive without warning and with their shallow draught, a crew of 70 and a payload of 80 tons get virtually everywhere by sea, firth and voe. It was inevitable that the Viking invaders would settle in Shetland and when their farmers colonised the land, transformed the landscape.

Did the Vikings totally extinguish the Celt influence? As one whose genes are half Viking through my Hardisty family, Yorkshire roots and half Celtic Cornish I instinctively feel that they did not.

The vigour of the Vikings largely created the Shetland we know today and their exploits are celebrated in the triumphant sagas. There are however, the whispers of a Celtic heritage to be found in the music and poetry of Shetland, preserved and intense though disguised in the dialect.

An Irish monk in the ninth century took time out from writing a Latin commentary on Virgil to pen this poem in Gaelic:

> *I and Pangur Ban my cat,*
> *'Tis a like task we are at:*
> *Hunting mice is his delight,*
> *Hunting words I sit all night.*

'Tis a merry thing to see
At our tasks how glad are we,
When at home we sit and find
Entertainment to our mind.

'Gainst the wall he sets his eye,
Full and fierce and sharp and sly;
'Gainst the wall of knowledge I
All my little wisdom try.

So in peace our task we ply,
Pangur Ban my cat and I;
In our arts we find our bliss,
I have mine and he has his.

A far cry from the sagas, but not from, for example, Mary Ellen Odie's, "Da Sealkie Wifes' Sang" and other songs and poems which celebrate the unique aspects of life in the Northern Isles, the care of the land, the people and the wildlife which inhabit them.

Whin da first blink o day
Lights da grey sea wance more,
I creep fae my bed an geng doon ta da shore,
An dere be da Skerry i'da saatie sea-spray
I sing wi da Sealkie a sang ta da day.
Ooo-oo-oo etc
I sing wi da Sealkie a sang ta da day.

Whin da sun clims da sky
An da Sealkies maan go,
Dey leave me ta greet be da side o da Voe.
Bit dir voices I hear trowe da soond o da sea
"We'll come back, Sealkie-wife, fir we're waitin fir dee."
Ooo-oo-oo etc
"We'll come back, Sealkie-wife, fir we're waitin fir dee."

Dan da last light o day
Laeves da rim o da sea,
An waves on da shingle maks music ta me.
A'll be doon be da Skerry i'da Mon's silver light
Ta sing wi da Sealkie a sang ta da night
Ooo-oo-oo etc
Ta sing wi da Sealkie a sang ta da night

A NOTE ON SOME HISTORICAL ACCOUNTS OF THE EAST MAINLAND OF SHETLAND, WHALSAY, BRESSAY, OUT SKERRIES AND NOSS

Lerwick has attracted the attention of every visitor and most travel writers also made it to Noss, Bressay and Whalsay. The delights of Nesting, Lunnasting and Delting gradually come to be appreciated and the advent of Sullom Voe Oil Terminal brought all these areas into sharper focus. My old chemistry master, Freddie Field at Kingswood School wrote to me about his visit, "I understand you have been posted to Shetland. My wife and I honeymooned in the islands and took passage on a ship (I believe called, 'the *Earl of Zetland*') and sailed from Lerwick up the east coast. We had thick fog all the way up and all the way back, but the food on board was excellent and the chef's speciality was devilled kidneys. When friends asked me about our trip, I had to reply that I had seen little of the islands, but I can spot a good devilled kidney now without any problem."

John Brand (1701) noted with dismay that following the wreck of the ship *Carmelas* of Amsterdam in 1664, "they say for 20 days after the inhabitants of the Skerries drank liberally of the strong liquors driven ashore in casks."

Thomas Gifford (1733) described Nesting and Lunnasting, "It is all mountains and moffes, many fresh water lakes and burns with plenty of trouts in them; the inhabitants are for the most part fishers, as they are also on the island of Whalsay."

Sir Walter Scott (1814) landed at Lerwick after a rough voyage and feeling, "like a wet and weary sea-sick minstrel", but went on to enjoy himself immensely.

Samuel Hibbert (1822) admired what we would consider today a most unlikely place, "Rova Head – at this place nothing could well exceed the raggedness of the coast, the rocks being formed of immense boulder-stones cemented by the intervention of smaller fragments." He was captivated by "troops of shags who seem to consider themselves the garrison soldiers of all the small isles."

Reverend Samuel Dunn (1823) 2nd February: "When I landed (at Lunna) I was completely exhausted and wet to the skin, but knew not where to go. I found out a cottage, immediately took off my clothes, lay down on a straw bed and slept soundly until nearly seven, when I arose and preached. I told the people I would meet privately those who were concerned for their soul's salvation … seven remained."

"Two Eccentrics", (1831) came to Shetland to walk and also found the weather particularly challenging, "We were hurled before the wind like perils on a blast of hell, through quagmire and bog – up hill and down brae."

Christian Ployen (1840) the Danish Governor of the Faroes, was an intrepid traveller who visited Dales Voe and Laxfirth. He reported, "The houses are substantial and the fields are prettier than any other in all Shetland." He made the crossing to the holm on the Cradle of Noss: "Accustomed to high rocks and convinced by long experience that I am not at all subject to giddiness, I sprang instantly into the cradle and made the passage over to the holm. The sensation is interesting of hanging in mid air between the steep precipices surveying the foaming sea beneath." (The gap was 65ft wide!)

John Reid (1869) complained that visiting Noss involved, "having to walk to the other side of Bressay, I left the road and scampered on, over heath and bog and stony hill" to reach the ferryman's cottage – Here the wife, "mentioning in commendation of that worthy (her husband) pronounced, "he's a Shetlander, and nane o' thae Scotch bodies!"

Dr Robert Cowie (1871) reported that the natural arch in South Bressay, "The Giants Leg", was created by a giant who "in leaping from Shetland to Orkney, succeeded in getting one leg over, but left the other behind and here it still stands at the Bard of Bressay."

John Tudor (1883) observed that, "About Dales Voe (Delting) you pass spots that have a certain wild, weird picturesqueness of their own."

Dr Mortimer Manson (1932) on Whalsay enjoyed "beautiful and interesting views are seen from several vantage points;" he considered Gletness, "one of the prettiest parts of Nesting on account of the islands of different sizes lying off it."

Derek Gilpin Barnes (1943) saw wartime service at RAF Sullom Voe:- "the station lay like a sullen explorer's encampment by the deserted shores of a black and evil loch. Yet in that austere landscape, there was the utmost beauty as well as forbidding gloom. One sensed that the noise of aircraft and the prolonged shouting of men were but a momentary echo in the long, northern silence that would again irrevocably descend."

A. Alvarez (1983) the poet, undertook a 'North Sea Journey' as oil production developed offshore and the oil was piped to Shetland. "It is characteristic of the Shetlanders," he reported, "that the first to benefit when the (oil) money began to flow were the exposed and underprivileged." When he visited Shetland, "the sun shone without a break, the breeze was gentle and the thermometer hovered around seventy degrees – what in Shetland is a heat-wave. It was like Paradise with a temperate climate, silent and unpopulated and astonishingly beautiful. The intense activity (of Sullom Voe Terminal) seems to occur without human intervention, as if by magic. The terminal is as unpeopled as the Shetland landscape."

Jill Slee Blackadder (2003) rejoices in all Shetland and on the east side particularly highlights, "South Nesting, with its limestone bands beneath the ground surface, is full of tiny valleys, gorges, peaks and hollows. Vivid green fertile fields tuck themselves in between knolls and hummocks of limestone outcrops and a wealth of wild flowers gild the roadside verges in summer."

WALK 1: LERWICK MARKET CROSS – KEBISTER NESS – DALES VOE – WINDY GRIND

8 miles (13 kms) : 5 hours

Cycle/Car: Car to Windy Grind, cycle to Lerwick Market Cross, 5 miles (8 km)

OS Maps: Landranger Sheet 4 Shetland – South Mainland
Explorer 467 Shetland – Mainland Central

A walk of real contrasts with no difficult terrain. As the first part of the walk is through the busy commercial and industrial areas of Lerwick, the best day to do this walk is Sunday. There is a great deal to see in the town and time should be allowed for this on a non-walking day. Otherwise, admire the activity at the hub of Shetland and then enjoy the expanse and freedom as you strike out for Kebister Ness.

The Eastside Way starts with a quick burl round the market cross in the centre of Lerwick before heading down to Victoria Pier and heading north up the Esplanade. Toilets are available here. Note the guns at Fort Charlotte overlooking the fish market as the ferry terminal to Bressay is reached. The Albert Building (1900) which is home to the Lerwick Port Authority and LHD Marine Supply shop is convenient for any last minute outdoor clothing requirements. Turn right to pass in front of the Malakoff and go down some steps to reach the North Ness Business Park with its 'Gutters Hut', a reminder of the importance of Lerwick as a herring station in the early 20th century. At the end of the walkway is a memorial plaque to the eight men lost at the

The Ward Hill of Bressay, and Lerwick, from the N. of Fort Charlotte E.

From a water-colour drawing by Sir H. Dryden

15

Walk 1: LERWICK MARKET CROSS – KEBISTER NESS – DALES VOE – WINDY GRIND

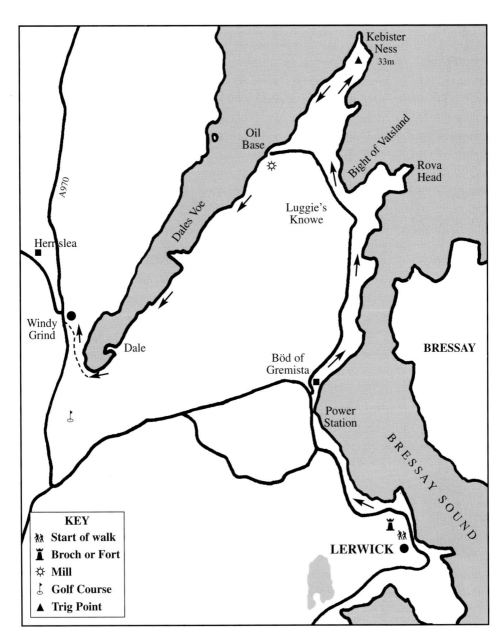

Kebister
Ness
33m

Bight of Vatsland

Oil
Base

Rova
Head

Dales Voe

Luggie's
Knowe

A970

Hernslea

Windy
Grind

Dale

Böd of
Gremista

BRESSAY

Power
Station

BRESSAY SOUND

LERWICK

KEY

🏃 Start of walk

♜ Broch or Fort

☼ Mill

⚑ Golf Course

▲ Trig Point

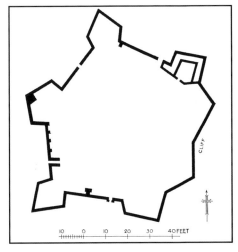

Plan of Fort Charlotte, Lerwick.

Anglo-Scottish pier explosion on 2nd November, 1943.

Go up Browns Road to join Commercial Road and return to the sea front down Garthspool Road. Walk on to pass the Holmsgarth ferry terminal and just before the power station at Gremista is reached, admire the gardening efforts displayed around a bungalow – a great variety of trees and bushes.

Gremista has a major road junction and we leave the main road (A970) to head north round the Point of Scotland. Before doing so find time to visit the Böd of Gremista which is an 18th century fishing booth, beautifully restored to reflect its role as a work place and birthplace of Arthur Anderson, joint founder of P&O shipping company. The helpful curator gives excellent tours round the building.

Follow the road past Shetland College, The Shetland Times and other businesses and finally the Greenhead Base. The road is aiming for the Dales Voe service base, but we are going to leave it shortly after passing the entrance to the SIC recycling plant at Rova Head. Note a natural arch and then at a sheep fold near the top of the hill, turn right through a metal gate and walk across to the Bight of Vatsland. The Holms of Vatsland lie offshore, but its stacks are close to an extensive croft

Clive Henderson, Curator of the Böd of Gremista, Lerwick.

17

Kebister Armorial Stone.

Mill and burn, Kebister.

ruin with its own private beach. The small cliffs have little secret caves in them and one can now really enjoy being in open country. Climb up to the Trig Point (33m) on Kebister Ness and take in the views before descending to Doos (dove) Cove.

Above us is the hill named Luggie's Knowe, on the abrupt peak of which once lived a wizard of that name. Luggie brought up fish ready cooked in some subterranean fire through a hole in the knowe. John Brand (1701) thought, "this was certainly done by the agency of evil spirits, with whom he was in contact." Sadly, Luggie was convicted of sorcery and burnt to death on Gallow Hill, Scalloway.

Further along the coastline there is a security fence round the service base – climb into the hill round it and descend back to the coastline by two ruined buildings by a burn. An archaeological excavation here in 1985 showed that one of the buildings was a tithe barn belonging Henry Phankouth, Archdeacon of Shetland in 1500. An ornate armorial stone which had been placed over the door was recovered during the dig and can be seen in the Shetland Museum. The area has been uninhabited since 1817.

A change of terrain means that the lush grazing land becomes heathery slopes, but take time to explore a deep geo with a water mill ruin in the delightful burn above it. You will not be able to resist the temptation to stroll on the green sward of Muckle Ayre and the banks of the Lees end with a curved tombola and a marshy area between the voe and the golf course. Aim for a bridge across the vadill – the burn is popular with herons – and gain access to a green road which heads up to the Windy Grind. Pass a derelict croft with interesting arched windows before reaching the two stiles, access to the A970 and layby.

If in need of refreshment, it is but a few minutes stroll to cross the road and take the hill down to Veensgarth and The Herrislea House Hotel.

WALK 2: WINDY GRIND (DALE) – GOTT ▬▬▬▬

9 miles (15 kms) : 8 hours

Cycle/Car: Car to Gott, cycle to Windy Grind (nearly opposite the junction of A970 and B road to Veensgarth), 1.5 miles (2.5 km)

OS Maps: Landranger Sheet 4 Shetland – South Mainland
Sheet 3 Shetland – North Mainland
Explorer 467 Shetland – Mainland Central

The waters of Dales Voe and Lax Firth dominate this walk, the highlights of which are Fora Ness and Hawks Ness. Road option between Califf and Breiwick.

At Windy Grind cross the stile and walk down the 'green road', the former track to Lerwick. The start of the walk is clear of the golf course where the greens vie with the pasture land. The croft land has many stone clearance cairns whilst the island of Green Holm dominates the horizon north east. There is a stone marker on the cliffs opposite a fish farm raft and a ruin where the first houses come into view. A small shingle beach leads us round a knoll to a stile over a wooden fence. South Califf stands at the road end and shares with North Califf fine sites above the Holm of Califf.

Pass a beach with a noost and a winch and then the going gets a little tricky and may involve coming inland for a short stretch. Return to the shore where a solar powered horn has been erected and enter Breiwick, a wide shingle beach bay with several houses.

Fora Ness can now be enjoyed and walk to the cliffs of beautiful Fora Ness Voe. Above are two dry stone wall windbreaks and if it is sunny the sea is a wonderful azure colour. There is a small natural arch on the east side and distant views include Kesbister and Ander

Lamb, Califf.

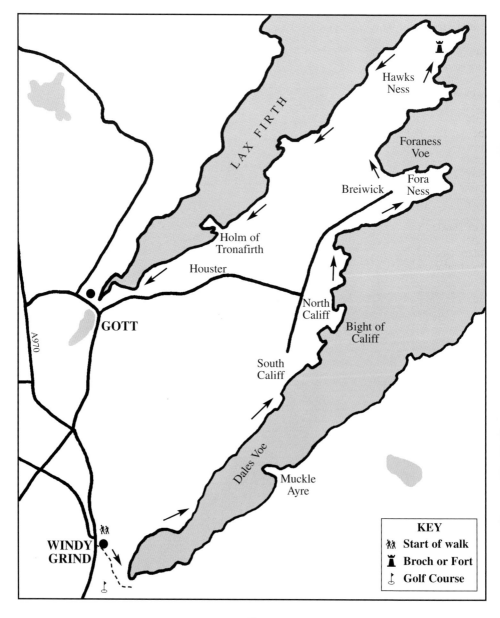

Hill on Bressay. A croft ruin will be found on the shoulder of the hill at Houbie, the last we shall find for a while. Brim Ness has a large cave and before descending to a valley with a pebble beach, note a planticrub. The Bight of Brimness has a notable "Gods Bridge", in this case, a natural arch going three ways. Sadly, the area also had sheets of metal from a 1980s barge wreck lying on the rocks.

We are now approaching Hawks Ness where a dry stone wall runs down from the headland to a small sheep pund. The stones in the wall would have come from the broch which stood on the high rocky knoll close to the edge of the cliff fence. Only part of the actual structure can be seen, but there is a single course of masonry. Overall diameter is about 55ft and there appears to have been a narrow opening in the wall towards the north east. This is a great place to sit and enjoy lunch with its view of South Nesting to the north.

Off Hawks Ness is the Unicorn Rock named after the *Unicorn* which was sent to capture Mary Queen of Scot's lover Earl Bothwell. A local pilot on board Bothwell's ship lured her on to the rock on 25th August, 1567 and it has been so named since then. Gordon Williamson identified the Unicorn Rock for me. In March 1990 he was on board the *Zenobia* when she ran full speed onto the north west corner of the Unicorn. She was fortunately towed off, leaving 30ft of keel and some side planks but lived on to sail again. So the Unicorn was not renamed *Zenobia*.

Next comes Laxfirth, another long voe with no immediate signs of human habitation on the east shore, though a sheep pund will be found by the distinctive Skerby Ayre made up of pebbles and home to a tern colony. As the Houb approaches, beyond the Holm of Tronafirth, make for a farm building on a track which connects with the public road. Follow the road past the SPCA, Shetland Oiled Bird Cleaning Unit, set up in the aftermath of the *Braer* oil tanker sinking in 1992. Note also a plantation of trees and a bird hide as you follow the road past houses (one with a stone otter in a landscaped stream) and cross the road bridge which stands between Lax Firth and Strand Loch, to complete this walk.

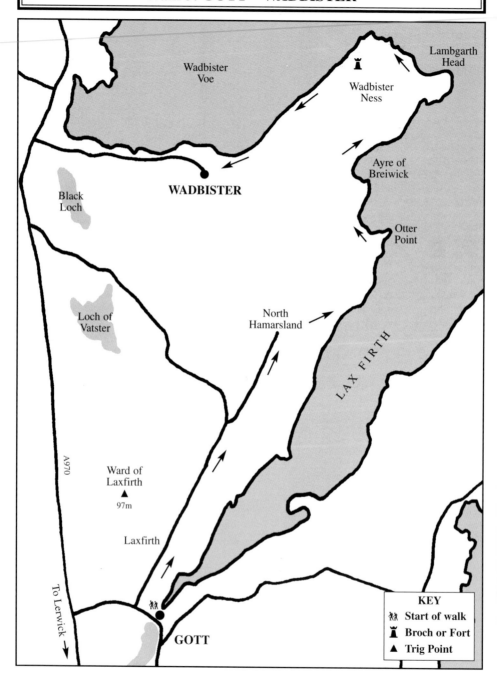

WALK 3: GOTT – WADBISTER ▅▅▅▅▅

5 miles (8 kms) : 3 hours

Cycle/Car: Car to Wadbister, cycle to Gott, 3.5 miles (6 km) via A970 or 3.5 miles (6 km) via A970 to Vatster, then unclassified road past Laxfirth to Gott

OS Maps: Landranger Sheet 4 Shetland – South Mainland
Sheet 3 Shetland – North Mainland
Explorer 467 Shetland – Mainland Central

A great walk round Wadbister Ness, much of it in open countryside before reaching the sheltered waters of Wadbister Voe and the well established trees in the garden of Wadbister at the road end.

Start the walk at Laxfirth Bridge, which crosses the waters coming down from Strand Loch to Laxfirth and climb up the road past the houses, one decorated with a fiddle and music notes and follow the unclassified road to Laxfirth. Some notable gardens can be enjoyed on the way, particularly Vadill View, all overlooked by the Trig Point 97m on Ward of Laxfirth.

Below on the shore stands the mansion, Laxfirth House, with its own pier and owned by the Leslie family. The former primary school for the area is now a workshop with three pointed windows and can be seen on the left-hand side of the road.

Leave the main road to follow the coastline or the long track to North Hamarsland where an extensive property enjoys an enviable position. From here bear north east to the shore at Otter Point passing a stone cairn; by the pebbly beach on the Ayre of Breiwick is a circular stone ruin.

Go round Lambgarth Head to reach the point of Wadbister Ness. The broch of this ness will be found a little way into Wadbister Voe on about the third rocky spur which juts out into the voe. Difficult to access, because of the jagged rock formation, most of this broch has been swept away by the sea, but enough remains to identify it.

Make your way south west across peat banks to reach a stone enclosure and wire fence. Cross a footbridge and reach the planticrubs which herald approaching dwellings. There is a splendidly restored stone building by a pebble beach with its own noost and winch. Ascend to and cross the field which lies between the shore and Wadbister house to end the walk where trees flourish at the road end. Like the garden of Kergord House in Weisdale, Wadbister has been, in the past, a popular place for wedding parties to be photographed.

Broch, Wadbister Ness.

Walk 4: WADBISTER – CATFIRTH

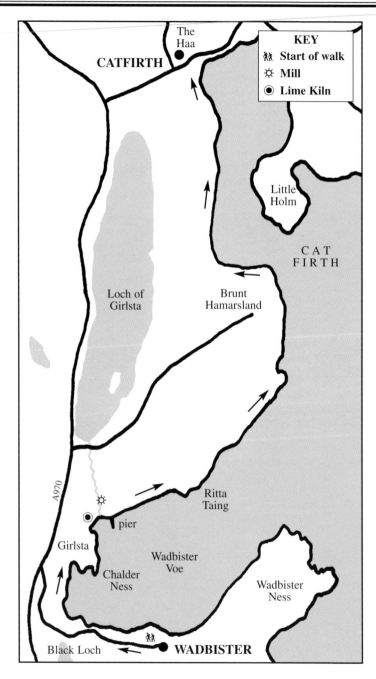

WALK 4: WADBISTER – CATFIRTH

5 miles (8 kms) : 3 hours

Cycle/Car: Car to Catfirth, cycle to Wadbister, 4 miles (7 km)

OS Maps: Landranger Sheet 3 Shetland – North Mainland
Explorer 467 Shetland – Mainland Central

If cycling from Wadbister the route takes one south on the A970, mainly on the west shore of Loch Girlsta. This is Shetland's largest and deepest loch with brown trout and Arctic char breeding here. Scottish Natural Heritage considered the char as being "a healthy indigenous population" when surveyed in 2003. The island to the south of the loch is, according to legend, the burial site of Geirhilda, a Norwegian princess who drowned in the loch in AD 870 whilst fishing for Arctic char. It is also the loch that a Lieutenant J. W. Pochin rode out to in October 1904, undressed, went into the loch and drowned. His body was recovered after a heavy charge of gun powder was exploded at the bottom of the loch. The explosion produced a violent concussion but no body at the time. It was later found floating in the water. Why Lieutenant Pochin went into the loch remains a mystery. Perhaps he was lured in to his doom by the siren voice of a phantom Geirhilda. A memorial stone (not visible from the road) stands on the loch's western shore. It reads: 'Near this spot Lieutenant J. W. Pochin RN HMCG, Lerwick, was drowned October 19th 1904'.

In 1905, two beautiful stained glass windows were placed in memory of him in a convent in Lerwick but were eventually moved and installed in St Magnus Episcopalian Church in Lerwick on 28th October, 1973.

At Girlsta take the road to its end at Wadbister. The house at Wadbister is renowned for its trees and garden and from here walk the road past houses, also with attractive gardens and a salmon farm service station. Cross a fence and walk down to the shore, then through a large metal gate to a small sandy beach. Pass a large stone-lined boat noost and a small bay with a

shingle ayre popular with sea birds. Cross the Burn of Chalderness and what resembles a miniature war-time pillar to reach a pebbly beach with a small standing stone commemorating members of the Turcan family.

At an area of industrial development a huge limestone kiln, now ruined, reminds us of the importance of limestone ash as a fertiliser in years gone by. The lime kiln was built in 1872 and was the only commercially operated one of its kind in Shetland. At its peak in 1912 the kiln was producing 350 tons of lime a year, mainly for agricultural use. It has now been

Pochin's monument, Girlsta Loch.
© Shetland Museum

acquired by Shetland Amenity Trust which plans to restore the structure.

On the banks of the burn flowing down from the Loch of Girlsta is a water mill ruin. At Girlsta Pier, built "for use by the community and visitors", progress along the shore of Wadbister Voe by heading for Ritta Taing. Near this point, which is almost opposite Wadbister, on a shoulder of Hill of Brunt Hamarsland, is a circular stone ruin similar to prehistoric settlements sites. Walk through scattered stones of an ancient sheep pund to cross a wire fence and a rocky knoll. Offshore are salmon cages and we are now in Catfirth. A delightful small cove with a shingle ayre will be found on the shore just before the first houses appear. A road connects these houses at Brunt Hamarsland with the main road near Girlsta. Beyond is a ruined house on the foreshore and a small shingle beach. A concrete slab helpfully acts as a footbridge towards another small croft ruin, this one with a crow's nest in a tree.

One is now walking the slopes of Long Hill, but one can choose to go down to the shore by going through a wooden gate at the end of a wire fence. A small croft ruin stands between here and Vallin Ness and a stretch of shingle beach. Catfirth can be so serene and beautiful. It is difficult to imagine it as a wartime military base, but naval bases were established here in both World Wars. At the end of World War I a small flying boat station was established at Catfirth to enable the RAF to operate maritime patrols in search of enemy submarines and to protect local convoys.

The walk ends by climbing up to the road where the Burn of Catfirth comes tumbling down the rocks to the sea. It is a most attractive waterfall feature, not because of its size but because it is so unexpected and a delight to discover. Aim for a metal gate in the fence to reach the road. The knoll above it is named Klingrahool after the roses which grew on it. A most fitting place to end this enjoyable walk.

Limekiln, Girlsta.

Siggys in profusion, croft, Catfirth.

Walk 5: CATFIRTH – GLETNESS (including Little Holm)

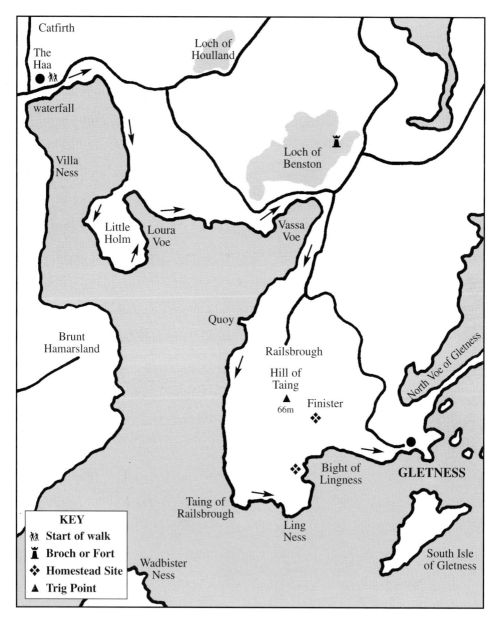

Catfirth

The Haa

waterfall

Loch of Houlland

Loch of Benston

Villa Ness

Little Holm

Loura Voe

Vassa Voe

Brunt Hamarsland

Quoy

Railsbrough

Hill of Taing

▲ 66m

Finister

Bight of Lingness

GLETNESS

North Voe of Gletness

Taing of Railsbrough

Ling Ness

Wadbister Ness

South Isle of Gletness

KEY
- 𝝅 Start of walk
- ♜ Broch or Fort
- ❖ Homestead Site
- ▲ Trig Point

WALK 5: CATFIRTH – GLETNESS (including Little Holm) ■■■■

5 miles (8 kms) : 3 hours

Cycle/Car:　　Car to Gletness, cycle to Catfirth, 4 miles (7 km)

OS Maps:　　Landranger Sheet 3 Shetland – North Mainland
　　　　　　　Explorer 467 Shetland – Mainland Central

A walk of contrasts; Catfirth is sheltered and the banks are small whilst at Gletness a more dramatic coastline awaits, with the scenic isles of Gletness lying offshore. Easy walking all the way.

Start the walk by crossing the road bridge near where the B9075 passes the turning to Catfirth Croft. Shetland poet, James Stout Angus, was born at The Haa which is near Klingrahool where the Burn of Catfirth cuts through a knoll and tumbles over a waterfall to the sea. There is a tree conservation area where a young oak looked pretty healthy and a small weekend cottage with a walled garden. A house nearly opposite, Andervilla, has a garden, particularly noted for the way the trees have been landscaped. Cross another footbridge, over the Burn of Quoy and cross the fence onto the shore line. The South Nesting shop and Post Office – Robertson and Read can be easily accessed for provisions from here.

Catfirth was a naval base during World War I & II and an RAF flying boat station at the end of World War I. Various buildings, all looking rather gloomy now, are set back from the shore. A rusting ship's propeller does little to cheer one up as we pass a large slipway and aim to cross Loura Voe by walking the causeway to Little Holm. There is a rocky knoll at the south end of the island which is a

Waterfalls, Burn of Catfirth.

good resting point to survey any mussel pickers at work at low tide. John Tudor reports that in August 1879 a large school of ca'ing whales were trapped and 108 were slain. At Christmas 1992, seven orca whales, three males and four females, stayed in Catfirth for nearly two weeks and many people came to view the pod. The massive dorsal fins were easily spotted from the shore. All the whales survived. Visitors were helped with up-to-date information by a local resident, Willie Hunter. Willie would also show, with pride, a letter from Winston Churchill he received after helping with arrangements for the Prime Minister's visit to North Africa in 1943.

Back on the mainland, pass a geo with a winch and a small shingle beach with three noosts and a little cairn on the headland. The primary school (soon to be relocated) stands between the Head of Vassa Voe and Loch of Benston, a loch popular with swans and noted for the broch site on the Holm of Benston with its traces of a submerged causeway.

A small jetty and marina has been established here as we head south. Note a small island about 60yds from the shore which has the remains of a ruined stone structure. Peat ashes, a stone axe and a stone lamp have been found in the ruins and an artificial causeway, some of it carefully built 2ft above the sea bottom, runs in a semi-circle to the shore.

Quoy boasts a large noost and an islet on which a narrow cairn has been built as a navigation aid. Above is the croft of Railsbrough, the Trig Point on the Hill of Taing (66m) and a pair of neolithic, oval house ruins near to the south west of the croft of Finnister.

On the shore line, pass a stone ruin and a concrete straining post of some grandeur opposite a salmon farm. Above the Taing of Railsbrough, the Ward of Bressay, Anders Hill and Noss all hove into view. At Bight of Lingness are two lovely shingle beaches, the second one has a notable prehistoric settlement site and at the time of the visit, a hatch from the ill-fated *Green Lily*. Cross a handy footbridge and a fine stile to reach the immensely attractive settlement of Gletness.

Quoy, Railsbrough, Catfirth.

WALK 6: GLETNESS – ESWICK

6 miles (10 kms) : 4 hours

Cycle/Car: Car to Eswick, cycle to Gletness, 4 miles (7 km)

OS Maps: Landranger Sheet 3 Shetland – North Mainland
Explorer 467 Shetland – Mainland Central

Gletness has got to be one of the most scenic spots in the British Isles. The walk from Gletness to Es Wick is a classic one with so much to see and appreciate with walking terrain which is rarely demanding.

From the road end at Gletness, near a small house, head for the shore by using three stiles to arrive at a pebble beach. Offshore the North and South Isles of Gletness, Stunger and Tainga Skerry, are just some of the eye-catching attractions with the lighthouse, Hoo Stack and South Skerry also visible. The first objective is to walk Gletness and by walking the rocky foreshore or on the verge of pasture

land, head out on the ness. It is a popular area for otters, but even if they are as elusive as ever, there is plenty of birdlife to enjoy. Halfway down the ness is a rocky section which is easily surmountable and at the point is a sheltered spot for a break.

Return on the north side with its great views of North Voe of Gletness and join the track coming from North House to the main road and leave it to go through a metal gate. In front of Saltayre well kept boats add to the picture and note a planticrub which appears to support a most healthy potato patch. Further along, pass square planticrubs and a stone ruin on the

North Isle of Gletness, Nesting.

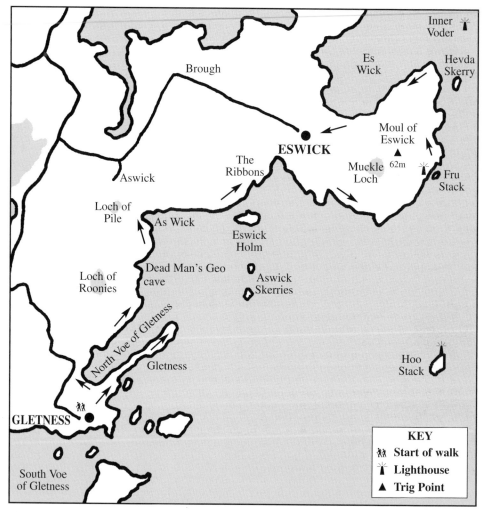

Inner Voder

Es Wick

Hevda Skerry

Brough

Moul of Eswick ▲

ESWICK

The Ribbons

Muckle Loch 62m

Fru Stack

Aswick

As Wick

Loch of Pile

Eswick Holm

Dead Man's Geo cave

Aswick Skerries

Loch of Roonies

North Voe of Gletness

Gletness

Hoo Stack

GLETNESS

South Voe of Gletness

KEY	
𝍌	**Start of walk**
⚲	**Lighthouse**
▲	**Trig Point**

shore edge. Almost opposite South Aswick Skerries is a cave, a geo which should be given a reasonable berth and then, the chilling Dead Man's Geo.

Descend to As Wick where the Loch of Pile is almost choked with marsh grass and head round a ruined fishing station to another pebble beach with a fairly large, rusting winch. Head east on the lower slopes of The Ribbans. You may be tempted to crawl through a sheep creep to get to a fence, to find two ruined stone punds with a short section of stone wall heading up the hill. Eswick Holm resembles a submarine and from the cliffs above it, noted for their waterfalls, round the south Bay of Eswick.

Head east again to climb up the slopes of Ward of Eswick and find a possible refreshment spot and a garden seat which sits stoically high on the cliffs – great view, but it can be breezy! Climb up round The Flaach below which is Fru Stack. The lighthouse is comparatively new and was constructed here when its predecessor went over the cliffs some years ago. Note to the north east offshore is Inner Voder with its navigation aid and nearer the shore, Hevda Skerry, popular with singing seals. Croo Geo boasts a cave which resembles a natural arch and from the rise above it head west round Es Wick.

The views, whether of Whalsay, Skerries, Bressay or of Ling Ness and the coast of South Nesting Bay are fine. Descend to cross a burn, pass a loose arrangement of stones and follow an ancient cart track to connect with the road end at Eswick.

Gletness, Nesting.

Walk 7: ESWICK – BRETTABISTER

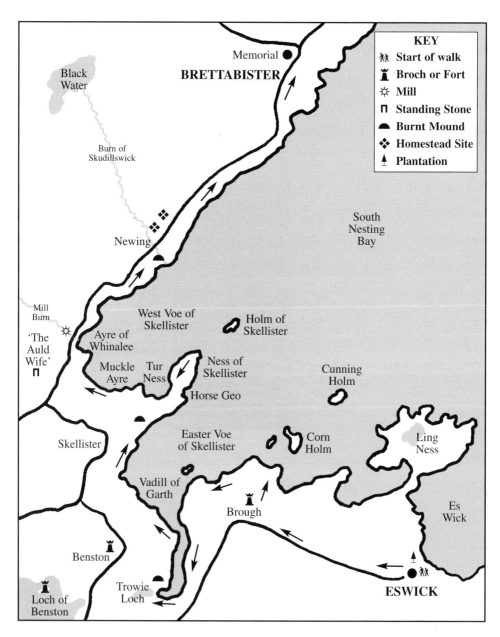

KEY

- 𝍢 **Start of walk**
- ♟ **Broch or Fort**
- ☼ **Mill**
- ⊓ **Standing Stone**
- ⬤ **Burnt Mound**
- ❖ **Homestead Site**
- ♠ **Plantation**

Memorial ●

BRETTABISTER

Black Water

Burn of Skudillswick

South Nesting Bay

Newing

Mill Burn

'The Auld Wife'
⊓

Ayre of Whinalee

West Voe of Skellister

Holm of Skellister

Muckle Ayre

Tur Ness

Ness of Skellister

Cunning Holm

Horse Geo

Skellister

Easter Voe of Skellister

Corn Holm

Ling Ness

Vadill of Garth

Es Wick

Brough

Benston

Trowie Loch

ESWICK

Loch of Benston

WALK 7: ESWICK – BRETTABISTER

6 miles (10 kms) : 4 hours

Cycle/Car: Car to Brettabister, cycle to Eswick, 5 miles (8 km)

OS Maps: Landranger Sheet 3 Shetland – North Mainland
Explorer 467 Shetland – Mainland Central

A walk through one of the most historic areas of Shetland with fine scenery, a bit of a tramp round the Vadill of Garth and always a chance of spotting a Nesting otter. The final two miles gives one the opportunity to explore a remarkable area of prehistoric houses and settlement areas near Newing.

The cycle ride takes one from Brettabister to the road junction B9075 with the unclassified road to Skellister and beyond. Broch remains which have been reduced to their foundations will be passed at Benston. About a mile to the north east at Brough is another broch site on a rocky knoll. Opposite the croft at Brough, the crofter, Donny Mackay, showed me a skew-put bearing a well-worn human head built into a now ruined cottage. It originally came from the Sinclair home, Old Haa of Brough, which was pulled down and the head is apparently a late 17th century carving.

The walk starts near the road end at Eswick. Here can be found the home of Terry Rodgers who has created a splendid plantation of mixed trees. Go through a metal gate and walk past the croft to cross a burn and arrive at the shingle beach of Es Wick. Climb west round a geo and reach a large boulder where there are extensive views of Ling Ness.

The walk round the coastline of Ling Ness requires access at all times to be agreed by the crofter. Otherwise, it is best admired from the road where the view includes the ruined croft house near the Loch of Lingness and the sandy beach, which is full of shells, can be clearly seen. To avoid crossing the ness return to the road by the plantation and walk it until returning to the coastline opposite Corn Holm. Cunning Holm and Linga Skerries draw near as you pass two ruined buildings and cross a

stone wall to reach the beach with its rusty winch.

Corn Holm has the remains of buildings on it and there is said to have been a broch on the island, but the evidence has almost entirely disappeared.

The banks of the foreshore have been buttressed by boulders and half way round East Voe, a well constructed U-shaped cairn acts as a 'tidy box' for items found washed up on the lovely beach.

Donny Mackay with stone carved head, Brough, South Nesting.

35

Standing stone of Skellister.

We now enter the dreaded marshy area at the narrow head of East Voe of Skellister and it is best to stick to the shore in order to keep ones boots dry. A small bathing hut actually turns out to be Donny Mackay's hen house where the flock is ruled by an extremely aggressive and protective cock. Note on the west bank a burnt mound and on the east bank, a ruined stone enclosure. Where the vadill narrows before joining Trowie Loch, you might save time by using the stepping stones to reach an old wooden gate in the west shore. Pass the burnt mound and two wire fences. The burial ground near Garth comes into view. There are no remains of the chapel that once stood here but built into the inner side of the north wall was a tombstone of late 17th century date commemorating "Thomas Sinclair who died 25th October 1688 and of his age the 19 yeare".

In the middle of the next bay are a large noost and a small standing stone by the fence. The Vadill of Garth presents no problems and we pass planticrubs and a tombola before reaching a wire fence, a burnt mound and a small section of wall which acts as a wind break. Pass Horse Geo to access Ness of Skellister. There is a small pebbly cove with five noosts and some boats. Round the corner spot a concrete otter trap ruin in a small offshore knoll. On rounding the head of the ness, there was great delight, then, in finding two otters who gave a great display on the rocks below before swimming off. On leaving the ness, before reaching Tur Ness, there is another decayed otter trap, this one of wood.

The beach at Muckle Ayre beckons, so cross this to climb up to the road, passing a ruined croft and by using two metal gates, watched by the Standing Stone of Skellister all the way.

Climb up to inspect this distinctive standing stone, known fittingly as 'The Auld Wife'; at certain angles she appears to be wearing a cloak which is falling off her shoulders. She stands 3 metres tall and is made of a pointed block of sandstone.

Most of the prehistoric sites are near the B9075 road as it aims for Brettabister. So, follow the road above the croft ruin and four well-built planticrubs. Above Ayre of Whinnalee is a house of that name and two burns romp down

Cairn, Hill of Skellister. Ness of Skellister beyond.

Homestead site? South Voe of Gletness.

Otter, Ness of Skellister, South Nesting.

the hill from Loch of Skellister. The Mill Burn once powered the ruined water mill, which is still standing by the road. The ruined croft at South Newing has well-maintained out buildings and 200 metres west of it is one small prehistoric house in a field system. Immediately east of the road, 100 metres east of the croft is another prehistoric house. Five hundred metres along the road at the foot of the road embankment is a circular site with numerous field walls. Walk on 170 metres further and near the east side of the road is an oval site, whilst 120 metres beyond this is another site beside the road on the east.

If you opt for the coastline at South Newing, then walk round a bluff with a stone enclosure on top of it and go through a metal gate down to a little bay popular with seals. Cross a wall to reach a pebbly beach with a loose stone boat noost and a sheep fold with a redundant wash behind it. There are field systems, outcrops and boulders galore and below two large planticrubs, a burn flows past a burnt mound site.

The war memorial at Brettabister comes into view. Take particular care round the geos at South Geo of Brettabister and climb up to the memorial to complete the walk.

East Voe of Skellister, South Nesting.

WALK 8: BRETTABISTER – BILLISTER ▪▪▪▪▪▪▪▪

7 miles (12 kms) : 4 hours

Cycle/Car: Car to Billister, cycle to Brettabister, 3 miles (5 km)

OS Maps: Landranger Sheet 2 Shetland – Whalsay
Explorer 467 Shetland – Mainland Central
Explorer 468 Shetland – Mainland North East

One of the finest stretches of coastline on the Eastside, for it includes some notable prehistoric fortifications and wonderful cliff scenes. Easy terrain with only one difficult area at The Groot.

If cycling one can enjoy one of the finest views of the islands before descending the hill down to Brettabister from Kirk Ward. Climb up to the cairn (a World War I watch tower) east of the road, shortly after passing Loch of Kellister.

The red granite and marble monument created in memory of the seven men of North Nesting, who gave their lives in the Great War 1914-1918 and the three in World War II 1939-1945, stands above the junction at Brettabister for Laxo and Housabister. From the monument, walk north east down to the Church of Scotland church behind which are the remains of a broch. The broch originally measured about 220ft in circumference at the outer wall. An enormous number of stones were used in the construction and the church is almost wholly built from stones of the broch. The broch was in a good position, being near the top of the cliffs and virtually unapproachable from the sea. The ruin that can be seen is in the shape of a conical mound about 70ft in diameter at the base.

A burn flows down from the Loch of Kirkabister beside which are the remains of a burnt mound.

Walk through Kirkabister past a burial ground and medieval chapel site (St Olaf) and leave the road to climb Hill of Neap. As you walk down the northern slopes, enjoy excellent views of Hog Island with its natural arch and

adjacent Stang Hog. There is no access to Hog Island but on the landward side of the narrow channel between the coastline and the island, three ramparts remain of an iron-age promontory fort which has been cut off by the sea. A central entrance gap can be seen in the ramparts. Above, are the derelict Haa of Neap and the former Church of Scotland manse, a place which Dr Cowie thought, "a more suitable site for a lighthouse than a manse."

Pass a derelict croft and head north up the coast with excellent views of Whalsay. Seli Geo and Teisti Geo are particularly pleasing, but The Groot is horrible. Here the sea almost reaches the Loch of Stavaness and if the tide is in, it is probably better to head south round the loch then climb north to a prominent cairn and then back to the cliffs, Even with the tide out it is tricky getting across the slippery boulders and I ended up with bruises to prove it. Never mind, the oyster catchers love the area as do the terns.

Stava Ness ("a fine walk", Dr Mortimer Manson) is a recorded broch site, but no trace

Broch ruin, Housabister. Hill of Neap beyond.

Walk 8: BRETTABISTER – BILLISTER

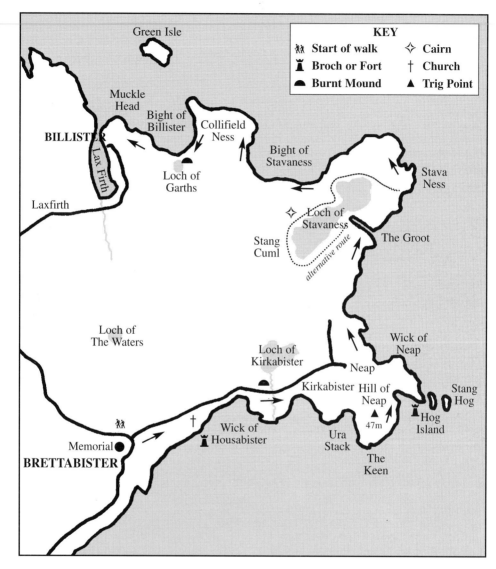

KEY

👣 **Start of walk**   ✧ **Cairn**

🗼 **Broch or Fort**   † **Church**

⬛ **Burnt Mound**   ▲ **Trig Point**

Green Isle

Muckle Head

Bight of Billister

Collifield Ness

BILLISTER

Lax Firth

Bight of Stavaness

Stava Ness

Loch of Garths

Laxfirth

Loch of Stavaness

Stang Cuml

alternative route

The Groot

Loch of The Waters

Loch of Kirkabister

Wick of Neap

Neap

Kirkabister

Hill of Neap

Stang Hog

▲ 47m

Hog Island

Wick of Neap

Memorial ●

†

Wick of Housabister

Ura Stack

Hog Island

BRETTABISTER

The Keen

---

of it now remains, however, there are other sights to be enjoyed. The Bight of Stavaness has a stone tombola by a ruin and some superb boulder beaches. In summer one can watch the terns mobbing Arctic skuas with both birds giving fantastic displays of aerobatics. An electricity line landfall sign, reached by crossing a boulder bridge, indicates where power goes under the sea to Whalsay on Collifield Ness. Presumably, there were fishing stations here, but now it is salmon farms which lie in Dury Voe. Green Isle is quite distinctive and out at sea the Whalsay ferries will often be seen passing each other in opposite directions.

Laxfirth and Billister are now in view and round the Bight of Billister is Loch of Garths, at the west end of which is a burnt mound, much damaged by water and excavation by rabbits. Pass a croft ruin on Muckle Head before crossing two helpful stiles to reach a modern jetty. It replaced the jetty commemorated by a concrete plaque complete with Viking galley and reading:

Zetland County Council
Billister Pier
1956

This used to be the ferry terminal for Whalsay. The walk ends here; there is a convenient public telephone box at Quoys.

The Groot, Stavaness, Laxfirth.

WALK 9: BILLISTER – LAXO

8 miles (13 kms) : 5 hours

Cycle/Car: Car to Laxo, cycle to Billister, 5 miles (8 km)

OS Maps: Landranger Sheet 2 Shetland – Whalsay
Explorer 468 Shetland – Mainland North East

An easy-going stroll round two nesses and a straight forward run in to Laxo, with the option of keeping to the road or taking the shore line. The shore line is well worth following, particularly, for the final mile.

From the public telephone box at Quoys in Billister, follow the road round the extensive marshy vadill area of Lax Firth to a concrete bridge. Cross it and leave the road to walk through giant iris and climb to The Heights

Walk 9: BILLISTER – LAXO

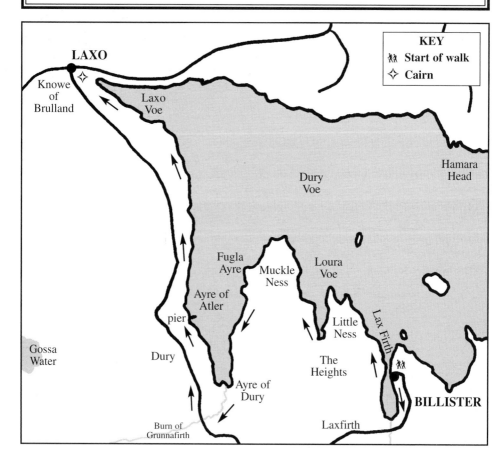

Plantation, Billister, Dury Voe.

Prehistoric cairn above burn at head of Laxo Voe.

above Lax Firth's western shore. An attractive copse of trees nestles by the water below a croft ruin. Walk round Little Ness and into Loura Voe, which appears to be far deeper than you might have thought and then, take on Muckle Ness. Fugla Ayre is the only significant feature of this ness, but the Ayre of Dury presents an extremely marshy area with no easy way round the coastline.

Go through a gate, cross a stile over a wire fence and follow the robust Burn of Grunnafirth to a bridge over which the B9075 road crosses. Walk the road north, noting at Dury a large kale yard adjacent to the croft. Atler Burn, with its attendant planticrubs, is passed and a road down to the salmon farm pier at Ayre of Atler. Traverse the heath to the shore line at Berry Geo and walk down below South Taraget to a glacial mound. Cross the Burn of Taraget by a footbridge and reach the head of Laxo Voe where the ayre almost seals the head of the voe. Here the waters of three burns, Mill, Seggie and Laxo converge and

wading the narrow channel is not recommended. Pass a tiny pier, home to wrens, to view the water cascading over the rocks by a small plantation of bushes and access the road by a stile. Cross the bridge to complete this section; the distinctive house at the junction of the B9075 and B9071 roads is named Windrush. At one time this was the home of the water baliff and was known as Laxo cottage. A prehistoric cairn below Windrush can be accessed by a small gate and there is a convenient mound within the large mound on which to sit and recover from the walk. The 'Inventory' describes the cairn as the Knowe of Brulland and its present height is about 10ft. Several large stones, one of which is set on edge, are exposed on the top. To me, it resembles the Thingsetter at Voe (11ft high), reputed to be the meeting place of the Thing of Delting, the ancient parliament. Perhaps, the Things of Lunnsting and possibly, Nesting, used to meet here (in the Isle of Man a grassy mound near Peel was the assembly field or Tynwald of the Man parliament).

WALK 10: LAXO – LUNNING

6 miles (10 kms) : 4 hours

Cycle/Car: Car to Lunning, cycle to Laxo, 5 miles (8 km)

OS Maps: Landranger Sheet 2 Shetland – Whalsay
Explorer 468 Shetland – Mainland North East

A walk that is full of variety and interest with the coastal scenery more dramatic once Hamara Head is reached. The aspect and poignancy of Bonnidale may be appreciated by many. Good possibility of otter and seal sightings.

Start this walk at the junction of the B9071 and B9075 roads at Laxo, where stands the prominent house named Windrush. The pre-historic cairn, known as the Knowe of Brulland, is a useful pre-walk refreshment spot and can be accessed by a small gate. It is a 10ft high mound with several large stones exposed on the top.

Walk the B9701 east and at a Viewing Point

enjoy the sight of the waterfalls at the head of Laxo Voe. Turn right to Laxo Terminal for Whalsay ferry (toilets can be found here) – the terminal the ferry operates from, unless weather conditions favour the use of Vidlin.

From the terminal car park cross a fence and walk the pebbly foreshore; progress may be laboured, but it avoids grazing land and attendant fences. From the Point of the Horn, climb onto the banks and near the croft at Tua, note a small mound with a ruin on it, perhaps the skeo of Skeo Taing. There are possible prehistoric homestead sites near Skelberry. At Sigga Taing, four otters emerged one after another from rocks in the cliff top to disappear down to the sea. Watch out for Omans Geo – it

Standing stone, Lunning.

45

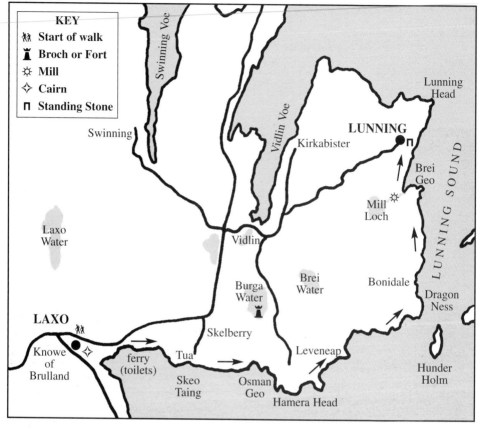

KEY
- 𝘹𝘹 **Start of walk**
- ♜ **Broch or Fort**
- ☼ **Mill**
- ✧ **Cairn**
- ⊓ **Standing Stone**

Swinning Voe

Vidlin Voe

Swinning

Lunning Head

LUNNING ⊓

Kirkabister

LUNNING SOUND

Brei Geo

Mill ☼ Loch

Laxo Water

Vidlin

Brei Water

Bonidale

Dragon Ness

Burga Water ♜

LAXO 𝘹𝘹

Knowe of Brulland ● ✧

ferry (toilets)

Skelberry

Tua

Leveneap

Hunder Holm

Skeo Taing

Osman Geo

Hamera Head

---

is the first high-cliff geo for some time and one can become complacent. Walk over the pebbly beach at Muckle Ayre and a cleaner and smaller beach further on. From here climb up to Hamara Head where there is a track going inland to Leevaneep. It is a dramatic headland and fortunately, a wire fence allows one to appreciate it safely. On the second headland two caves can be seen. Descend to the shore and note a well constructed noost quite high up above a small geo. Cross a wire fence to pass a fishing station ruin on the rocky foreshore. The electric power lines also head east past The Pow and climb Ward of Dragon Ness above Quilsa Taing. Beware sudden geos. Cross a pretty burn and climb over a rocky outcrop,

noting a cairn high on a hill to the north. Dragon Ness seems to be nodding to Hunder Holm and the several other islands between the Ness and Whalsay. Cross a fence and bid farewell to the power cable as it heads under the sea to West Linga and Whalsay.

People have enjoyed living in this area and there are ruined buildings, stone clearance cairns and above a shingle beach and sheep fold now broods the abandoned house of Bonidale. The life of the house was extended by colourful incomers after local people left – a fine family was raised here before the house was finally abandoned in the 1980s. The view from Bonidale includes Ward of Bressay,

Ander Hill, Noss, all of West Whalsay and Skerries. It must have been hard to give it up.

Cross a fence to a small wall above a geo and in the breeding season you may find black back gull chicks on their nesting area. A majestic cliff hoves into view, to reach it means crossing a tricky geo down which a burn flows. At Brei Geo, the burn flowing down from Mill Loch once powered two water mills. Cross a wire fence and pass three planticrubs to sit on the banks opposite Skerry of Lunning where seals frolic in the waves. The Standing Stone of Lunning is visible above to the right of a shed and can be easily reached by following a wire fence up from a winch on the shore to the point where the public road ends at Lunning. It is an irregularly shaped standing stone of quartz conglomerate which rises to a height of 6ft. It tapers towards the top. This stone marks the end of this walk.

Trig Point, Lunning Head. Lunna Ness beyond.

WALK 11: LUNNING – VIDLIN ■■■■■■

4 miles (7 kms) : 3 hours

Cycle/Car: Car to Vidlin, cycle to Lunning, 2 miles (3 km)

OS Maps: Landranger Sheet 2 Shetland – Whalsay
Explorer 468 Shetland – Mainland North East

A memorable walk round Lunning Head and Catta Ness with a small climb up from Ramna Geo and some outcrops above Orra Wick. Once clear of here there is a straight walk down to Vidlin.

Start the walk at the road end at Lunning and visit the standing stone which is over a fence on the east side of the road. It is an irregularly shaped standing stone of quartz conglomerate

Cairn, Dallican Water, Lunning.

which rises to a height of 6ft. It tapers towards the top.

Walk down to the coastline and the Skerry of Lunning, popular with seals, before heading over The Knowes to Ramna Geo. Aim north west up the slope to find a prehistoric homestead site on a lower slope which is easily identifiable but can get covered in bracken. It is well preserved, standing up to 3ft (1m) high and about 30ft (10m) in diameter. The thick wall surrounding the interior has traces of four alcoves. The entrance was on the south side.

Continue the climb past a distinctive white quartz rock to reach the Trig Point (65m) on top of Lunning Head. There are magnificent and extensive views from here and both the folly and the church of Lunna can be seen way to the west. Walk down to Mossie Geo, passing a distinctive boulder and on to the rocky beach at Orra Wick with its now redundant winch.

If opting for views, aim for a majestic cairn above Orra Wick by heading right of a small section of dry stone walling and cross a wire fence. Climb up through the grey and forbidding outcrops – as Jamie Jamieson said this is real Wild West territory and one expects Red Indians to be waiting round every bluff. Dallican Water is a delight with red-throated divers and rocks supporting lush vegetation.

At the cairn enjoy some time to identify features on Lunna Ness before rounding Catta Ness, Skeits Bay and the Taing, above which is a small stone enclosure. Distinctive Vidlin School can be seen down in Vidlin Voe; there are old peat workings to be crossed before meeting two wire fences. After the second fence is a ruined water mill, but although the

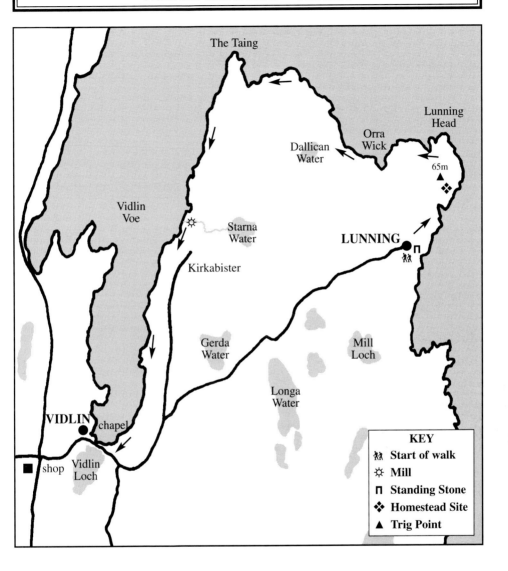

The Taing

Lunning
Head

Orra
Wick

Dallican
Water

65m

Vidlin
Voe

Starna
Water

LUNNING

Kirkabister

Gerda
Water

Mill
Loch

Longa
Water

VIDLIN chapel

shop Vidlin
Loch

KEY

🚶 **Start of walk**

☼ **Mill**

П **Standing Stone**

❖ **Homestead Site**

▲ **Trig Point**

grass is dark green, there is little water today coming down from Starna Water.

Walk through dense grass to the old croft at North Hill from which a track connects to the road at Kirkabister. Follow the road down to Vidlin, a most attractive place and end this walk at the head of the voe where there is a marina. Next to the marina is the delightfully situated Methodist Chapel which stands in a most commanding position. It will come as no surprise to know that this was once the site of a broch. Further on toilets will be found at the ferry terminal for Out Skerries and sometimes

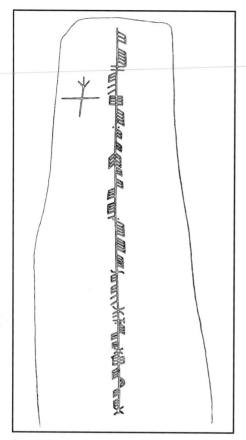

Lunnasting Stone, found locally, now in the National Museum. 3ft 8ins high with ogham script "King Nechtan of the kin of Ahehhtmnnn".

Whalsay. A well provisioned shop, John Herculson, is located at the junction of B9071 and the unclassified roads from Vidlin to Swinning and to Lunna.

The Lunnasting Stone was unearthed locally and is now in the National Museum. It is 3ft 8ins high with an ogham script translated to read, "King Nechtan of the kin of Ahehhtmnnn." How one wishes one knew more about these people and who exactly they were.

WALK 12: VIDLIN – LUNNA HOUSE ████████████

4 miles (6 kms) : 3 hours

Cycle/Car: Car to Lunna House, cycle to Vidlin Methodist Chapel, 3 miles (5 km)

OS Maps: Landranger Sheet 2 Shetland – Whalsay
Explorer 468 Shetland – Mainland North East

Our next objective is to walk Lunna Ness and I suggest it is done in three stages. The first stage is the shortest, but this allows time to explore both Vidlin and Lunna. Easy terrain.

There are a number of attractions in Vidlin, not least the smart public hall with a weather vane cock and the general store and post office, John Herculson, opposite it. A war memorial to 'The Brave men of Lunnasting' is prominent as are the Methodist Chapel and marina. The Cabin Museum, proprietor Andy Robertson, contains a fascinating collection of World War II memorabilia and will be found just past the Laxo ferry terminal on the left-hand side of the main road into Vidlin.

Vidlin Voe, chapel and school.

Andy Robertson in the Cabin Museum in Vidlin.

Walk the west shore of Vidlin Voe past the primary school with its aero generator and the ferry terminal (toilets) to Whalsay in certain weather conditions and Out Skerries on certain days.

Pass a salmon farm pier and round Vidlin Ness to catch up with the road at the head of Gunna Voe where there is a shingle beach. On the road a sign advises, "Antiques at end of road", whilst high above, the cairn on South Hill of Lunna (86m) is prominent. South Grinds has a riot of trees including oak. The coast route goes past the offshore Stack of Hellam to reach East Lunna Voe. Time now to explore the impressive walls of the walled garden and perimeter of Lunna House. This 17th century mansion, built by the Hunter family, can be reached by climbing up the slope in front of it. "This quaint and old fashioned, but most comfortable and commodious mansion occupies a commanding position ... never was a more romantic site chosen," thought Dr Robert Cowie in 1871.

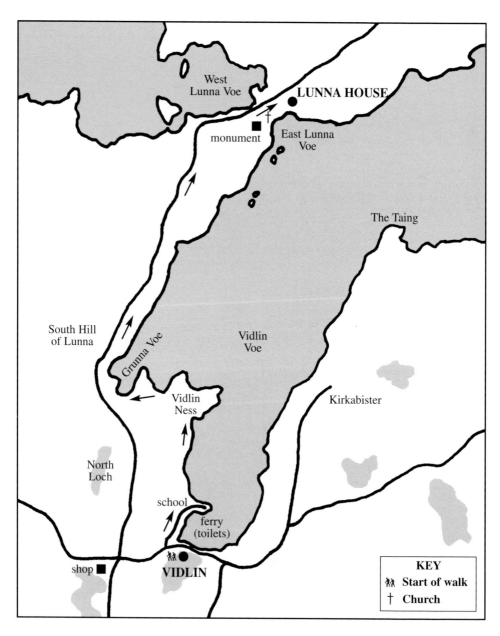

West
Lunna Voe

LUNNA HOUSE

monument

East Lunna
Voe

The Taing

South Hill
of Lunna

Grunna Voe

Vidlin
Voe

Vidlin
Ness

Kirkabister

North
Loch

school

ferry
(toilets)

shop

VIDLIN

KEY
Start of walk
† Church

Lunna folly. Skeo Ness and West Lunna Voe beyond.

Hunter's Monument, Lunna Kirk. Folly beyond.

To the left of the door is a stone with the arms and names of Thomas Hunter and Grisella Bruce who were married on 17th June, 1707. Evidently, the Hunter family engaged in smuggling activities, so it was quite appropriate that Lunna House was the original head-quarters of the World War II "Shetland Bus", an operation which involved smuggling people and supplies for the Norwegian resistance movement. By the door is a plaque to the memory of Leif Andreas, "Shetlands Larsen", the most decorated combatant (British and Allied) of the entire war. The 'Bus' operated from Lunna until its position became untenable due to enemy activities and so operations were transferred to Kergord House in Weisdale.

Terry and Helen Erwood offer bed and breakfast facilities to visitors and Lunna is a most interesting home to stay in. Originally built in 1660, it has been added to at various times giving it a somewhat rambling and secret interior. The 'Larsen Suite' has a romantic four-poster bed popular with honeymooners.

From the house descend in front of it and climb up to a folly built like a sentry box of stone. There are stone steps either side of it and great views. Walk down past a ruined building like a chapel, a former monastery, to the gate of Lunna Kirk or use the stone stile. It is the oldest church still used in Shetland, built in 1753 on the site of an earlier mausoleum and there were special celebrations to mark its 250th year in 2003. Two inscribed memorials to the Hunter family from the mausoleum are built into the porch; note also the large gallery accessed by stone steps and a leper window. It was the first church on this site but the remains of buildings survive on the Chapel Knowe (St Margaret), a rocky grass-covered knoll on the narrow isthmus between East and West Lunna Voes.

Lunna House from the south.

Armorial panel, Lunna House.

Early Iron Age pottery has been found on this site, which may once have also been a broch site.

The burial ground includes a memorial to ten crew of the Norwegian ship, *Hop* from Bergen, who gave their lives when the ship was torpedoed on 4th February, 1940. There is also a memorial to David Howarth (1912-1991) of the 'Shetland Bus' fame. He requested that his ashes be cast on the waters of Lunna Bay.

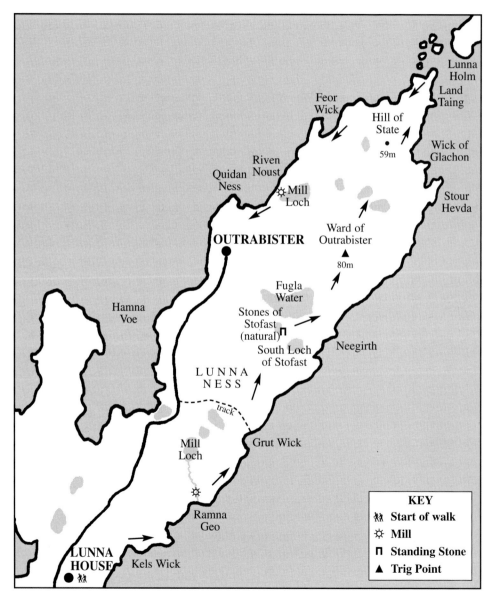

Lunna
Holm

Land
Taing

Feor
Wick

Hill of
State

Wick of
Glachon

Riven
Noust

Quidan
Ness

59m

Mill
Loch

Stour
Hevda

Ward of
Outrabister

OUTRABISTER

80m

Fugla
Water

Hamna
Voe

Stones of
Stofast
(natural)

South Loch
of Stofast

Neegirth

L U N N A
N E S S

track

Mill
Loch

Grut Wick

Ramna
Geo

KEY

🚶 **Start of walk**
☼ **Mill**
Π **Standing Stone**
▲ **Trig Point**

**LUNNA
HOUSE**

Kels Wick

WALK 13: LUNNA HOUSE – OUTRABISTER ███████████

7 miles (11 kms) : 5 hours

Cycle/Car: Car to Outrabister, cycle to Lunna House, 3 miles (5 km)

OS Maps: **Landranger Sheet 2 Shetland – Whalsay**
               Explorer 468 Shetland – Mainland North East

A walk into the wildest area of Lunna Ness and the stretch from Ward of Outrabister round the point of Lunna Ness should only be undertaken in fine weather. The terrain can be demanding, but there is a great deal to enjoy whether it be the landscape, the birdlife or possible sightings of otter.

Leave Lunna House by following a well defined track to the right of the entrance, admiring the carpet of wild flowers and probable sight of gannets diving into the sea. Cross a stone stile by a knoll and look down on Ramna Geo – great care is needed whilst walking round it. Great boulders are strewn both on the hillside and shore line, where there are ruins of a water mill beside the burn flowing down to the sea from Mill Loch. At Grutwick, note a particularly large boulder but not visible, is the Ninian pipeline, 36 inches in diameter carrying crude oil from East Shetland Basin oil fields. It makes its landfall here and heads for Sullom Voe Terminal across Lunna Ness. Since it commenced operations in 1978 over 2.6 billion barrels of oil have flowed through it.

Grutwick, Lunna.

Mill Loch, Lunna.

South Loch, Stofast Stones beyond.

Stones of Stofast.

A well-made track goes up from the beach (built for pipeline trenching plant to access the bay) and when a defunct quarry is reached, leave the track and return to the cliffs. Cross a wooden stile over a fence and a burn popular with snipe to reach a sheep fold. Climb up past the quartz boulders which guard the approach to the massive 2,000 tonne glacial erratic boulder split in two by frost named, the Stones of Stofast. They stand near South Loch of Stofast and from here climb up to Fugla Water, with its distinctive islet, to cross the large stone wall just before it enters the loch. Otter spraint (droppings) may be found here and there is a long wooden derelict otter trap alongside the wall. From the north side of Fugla Water climb up to the Trig Point on top of Ward of Outrabister (80m). Head north to the next hill on which is a solitary stone boulder. Four lochs now lie beneath one with Mill Loch on the east shore the largest. Aim for the west loch and keep inland from Stour Hevda and Wick of Glachon. The Hill of State (spot height 59m) is the next objective and it is quite steep in parts.

Descend to follow the valley north. On a tongue of land in the next valley is the ruin of a small house (a welcome sight). Descend the hill towards the coastline and find a sheep fold enclosure. We now lose the views of Whalsay and Skerries, but gain those looking north, including Fetlar and Saxa Vord on Unst.

From the Point of Lunna Ness the island of Lunna Holm seems very near. This Holm became a bit too near at 12.15pm on 26th July, 1912, when the inter-island supply boat, the S.S. *Earl of Zetland*, ran aground on it in a fog. Many of the 90 passengers transferred to the island and by mid-evening, 60 of them had been rescued by Yell boats and taken to Burravoe. The *Earl* was also taken to Burravoe, refloated and eventually made it to Aberdeen for permanent repairs before returning to duty early in August.

Pass a small shingle beach and walk Scord Dale to Feor Wick. Just before Riven Noust is a mill ruin beside the burn coming down from Mill Loch. Go through a metal gate and pass a shingle beach and a stone wall at the end of a fence. The Trig Point on Ward of Outrabister is clearly visible south east, whilst to the north, the houses of Burravoe, Yell, particularly the Old Haa and Overby, can be spotted as well as the Stack of the Horse. Walk through lush pasture to arrive at Outrabister, a striking house built in about 1700 legend has, to provide accommodation for a member of the gentry with a personal problem. Frank Watt now uses an outbuilding to sell collectables and it is open all the year round.

Otter trap, Fugla Water.

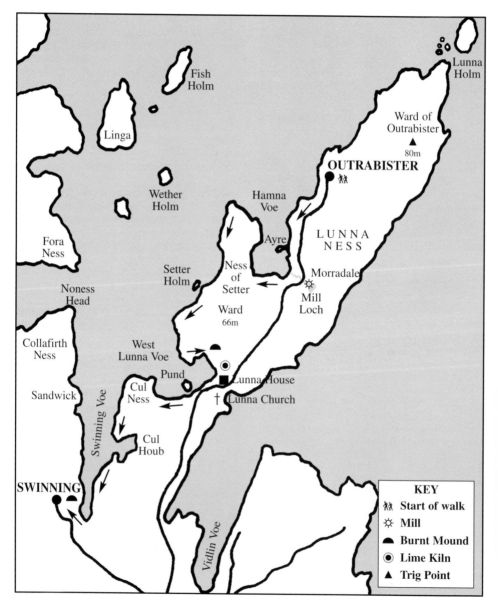

Fish Holm

Lunna Holm

Linga

Ward of Outrabister
▲
80m

OUTRABISTER
👥

Wether Holm

Hamna Voe

L U N N A
N E S S

Fora Ness

Ayre

Setter Holm

Ness of Setter

Morradale
☼
Mill Loch

Noness Head

Ward
66m

Collafirth Ness

West Lunna Voe

Pund

Lunna House

Sandwick

Cul Ness

Lunna Church

Swinning Voe

Cul Houb

SWINNING

Vidlin Voe

KEY	
👥	**Start of walk**
☼	**Mill**
⬤	**Burnt Mound**
◉	**Lime Kiln**
▲	**Trig Point**

WALK 14: OUTRABISTER – SWINNING ███████████

10 miles (16 kms) : 5 hours

Cycle/Car: **Car to Swinning, cycle to Outrabister, 7 miles (11 km)**

OS Maps: **Landranger Sheet 2 Shetland – Whalsay**
                    Explorer 468 Shetland – Mainland North East

---

Some of the easiest terrain in Shetland, with few fences and no high cliffs, can be enjoyed on this walk. The coastline may lack dramatic features but enjoys superb vistas to the north and west. The cycle ride to Outrabister is hilly in parts.

Outrabister can shine brilliantly white and is in great contrast to the derelict crofts to be found along the shore as we strike out for Hamnavoe; here there is an old booth by an ayre which protrudes into Boatsroom Voe. There are salmon farms offshore, but it is the hens (and their fine hen houses) which may attract attention and at Mooradale, east of the road, is a water mill with a curved lintel.

A substantial jetty is used by the salmon farmers and after this, the remains of a turf-covered look-out will be passed. It is a marshy walk to a dry stone wall which leads down to a small sheltered beach. Climb up the slope of the hill to a circular stone cairn; another more substantial cairn will be found after crossing a fence. At the point of Ness of Setter are great views of Outrabister, whilst to the north the whole of South Yell from the Stack of the Horse near Burravoe to Ulsta and its ferry terminal can be seen. Mossbank and Ronas Hill can also be seen with the island of Wether Holm being strikingly green. Behind it the gorge known as Neap dominates the east coast of Fora Ness.

Crossing from the ayre at Cul Houb, Swinning Voe.

Scramble over long, overgrown peat banks with a round stone enclosure opposite a salmon farm. By the islet of Setter Holm is a shingle beach with a cable hut for use by the farm. After rounding Grames Ness, the folly above Lunna House comes into view and from Skeider Taing, make for the shingle ayre which leads out to Skeo Ness with its large stone enclosure. Climb round West Lunna Voe to go through two gates along a track. Leave it to go down grazing land to a gate in the wall on the water edge near a very large burnt mound. Admire the work put into the construction of a lime kiln and a plantation of trees before passing a jetty, also used for salmon farm boats. In the next field is a magnificent ladder stile over a large dry stone wall which helps cross to an area for looking after sheep. A small island has been used as a pund and is accessible west at low tide. Stone buttresses on its east shore prevent sheep wandering from this end. Other sheep enclosures are on the mainland shore which are passed to reach shingle beaches below a small croft ruin. Cross an ayre to reach Cul Ness.

The Ninian Pipeline, having come underground from Grut Wick now goes sub-sea again to Swinister and two metal pulleys set in concrete and two diamond marker posts signify its presence.

We are now walking Swinning Voe and the prehistoric homestead site on Noness Head and the old croft at Sandwick are, in turn, visible.

The impressive ayre at Cul Houb should be walked round unless you don't mind paddling. I think its worth giving ones feet a bathing; note on the raised, green ground at the end of the ayre two small stone cairns 22yds apart – presumably once the Houb cricket pitch.

Then, it's off with the boots and best to follow the sheep route onto gravel sandbanks to cross the burn flowing fast to the sea.

Another ayre is passed on the approach to Swinning from which walk round the head of the voe to pass a small ayre, a noost with a jetty adjacent to it and a cordoned off burnt mound on the shore edge. Presumably, the large burn was once nearer to it. Cross this, admiring the willows as you do and take a green track from the shore to a metal gate and so reach the tree-canopied houses of Swinning.

WALK 15: SWINNING – COLLAFIRTH ███████

5 miles (10 kms) : 3 hours

Cycle/Car: Car to Collafirth, cycle to Swinning (a real challenge as it is 12 miles – 19 km with a hilly start)

OS Maps: Landranger Sheet 2 Shetland – Whalsay
Explorer 468 Shetland – Mainland North East

This walk includes the deserted settlement of Sandwick and a prehistoric settlement site. Quite easy to Sandwick but more of a challenge thereafter.

From the village hall in Vidlin take the road to Swinning and park at the road end on the right where a track leaves the main road.

Swinning is a delightful spot; a collection of houses which enjoy sheltered positions. There are a number of hornbeam and sycamore trees round North House whilst near Willie

Hughson's home is an avenue of willow. April is a fine month to explore this area and the lambing hadn't quite started though Willie had two lambs that day – a fortnight earlier than planned, "the ram got out early," he ruefully explained.

Follow the clear track along Swinning Voe to a small pier opposite a sand bar and cross a wire fence. There is an old sheep wash on the shore from which climb the heathery slopes of Flaw Hill to reach a green sheep track which heads north. We spotted our first wheatears of the

Sandwick, Swinning Voe, near Vidlin.

year before reaching a sheep fold opposite the distinctive tombola of Cul Houb. Descend the next gully to cross the Burn of Gluss and cross boggy pasture with a pallet bridge. Lunna House is now in view NE and to the north the islands of Wether Holm, Linga and Fish Holm. Sandwick nestles below the Hill of Sandwick and boasts an attractive beach with a large

Walk 15: SWINNING – COLLAFIRTH

DALES VOE

Noness Head

Gardaness Hill

COLLA FIRTH

Loomishun

Campberdown Hill
108m

Moastra

Treawick

Mill Burn

waterfall

Mill Loch

Collafirth Hill
150m

COLLAFIRTH

Hill of Sandwick
114m

Sandwick

Collafirth Burn

Clubba Water

Sandwick Burn

Cunnighill
176m

Flaw Hill
148m

Gluss Burn

SWINNING VOE

Longa Water

SWINNING

KEY
🚶 **Start of walk**
✧ **Cairn**
❖ **Homestead Site**

Sand Water

Sandwick, Vidlin.   **Bobby Tulloch**

stone enclosure behind it. To reach the beach, cross the burn (a wooden bridge has long since gone) and note the careful buttressing of the banks with stones.

From this beach we viewed a black back gull being angrily pursued by a bonxie. Wild iris grow in pastures here and from a marshy pool a disturbed female mallard flew. Leave the beach through a gate and pass a winch which bears a metal plate inscribed NMPJ Sept 1962. The initials belong to Pat Jamieson who was a friend of Laurie and Jean Morrison who were the last people to live in Sandwick and who left it in 1981. They died within two days of each other in 2002 and are buried together in Lunna Kirk. Their house, once thatched, is now a ruin though there is glass in some of the windows. The remains of a box bed is just visible under the rubble whilst behind the house a water pipe forlornly pokes out of the ground to drip into a large metal pot.

Continue on the track to pass Madge's Head and an attractive cove full of fulmars. The great surprise is provided by the waterfall near the bottom of Mill Burn. The water flows down a moss covered sheet of rock in a ravine carpeted with primroses inaccessible to the sheep. Go down to the shore to cross the burn and follow the sheep track again.

There is quite a rough stretch to be walked but one can dawdle and view shags that have two well-used vantage spots where the grass is worn and the smell is niffy.

Beyond Moastra, cross a burn red with evidence of iron ore. The burn has flowed down past an ancient cairn, 400 yards up the

Teenie, Laurence and Jean Morrison.
Bobby Tulloch

Prehistoric cairn with upright stone, Noness Head, Collafirth Ness.

slope of the hill. Visit this ruinous cairn which appears to have been oval with a setting of small upright stones. On its west side is an upright stone 3ft 3ins high, set in a packing of small stones.

Prehistoric settlement site, Noness Head, Collafirth Ness.

From here, climb up to a large stone enclosure behind which is a well preserved, prehistoric homestead site. One of the stone cairns resembles a cromlech or quoit and it has a capstone, slightly askew, measuring about five and a half feet long. This cairn seems to have been the site then, of not only domestic habitation, but also burial.

Collafirth Ness ends at Noness Head with its panoramic views stretching from Outrabister on the NE to the Scatsta Airport beacon to the NW. Below us on Colla Firth, a salmon farm of round cages is serviced by what looks like the bridge of a scrapped ship.

Make your way along the banks past several ruined crofts to the settlement of houses at the road end at Collafirth. Note how the burn flows though the garden and under a bridge at the attractively painted Collafirth House.

WALK 16: COLLAFIRTH – DALE (DELTING) ▬▬▬▬▬

6 miles (10 kms) : 3 hours

Cycle/Car: Car to Dale, cycle to Collafirth, 5 miles – 8 km, mainly uphill

OS Maps: Landranger Sheet 2 Shetland – Whalsay
Explorer 468 Shetland – Mainland North East

An enjoyable stroll along Collafirth before a climb onto the ridge on Gardaness Hill where there is a well defined track all the way to Dale.

Leave the sandy ayre at Collafirth and cross the burn to climb diagonally north east in the direction of Breckon and Uphouse. There is a choice of shore edge or road for a short while – it ends at a gate where fuchsias and other plants display in profusion. Follow a track to another gate and descend to a ruined croft on the foreshore. Admire an impressive bridge/

stile to give the owner access to a potato patch. The track continues to more ruins and note the well constructed noost on the foreshore. Cross two wire fences and draw level with salmon cages on the voe. An extremely useful sheep track now helps one along and ahead Fora Ness begins to loom. At the point of entry to Colla Firth, three small standing stones would have told anybody in a boat which firth they were entering. Pass a ruined bothy and scramble round a tricky bit – sheep make it, so, so can we! Walk through an old wire fence and at the end of the Ness find a large stone

Croft ruin, Ube, Gardaness. Fora Ness beyond.

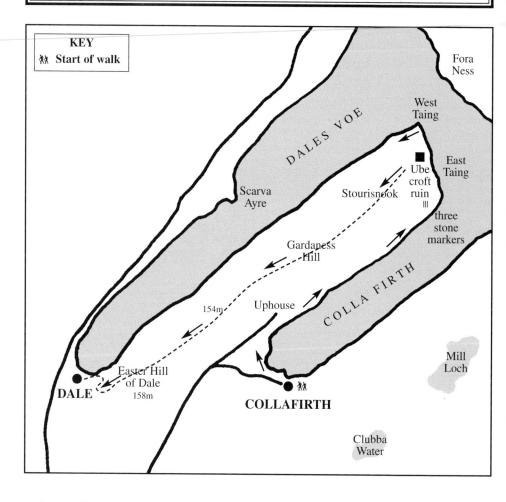

KEY

🚶 **Start of walk**

Fora Ness

West Taing

DALES VOE

East Taing

Ube croft ruin ‖

Scarva Ayre

Stourisnook

three stone markers

Gardaness Hill

COLLA FIRTH

Mill Loch

154m

Uphouse

Easter Hill of Dale

DALE

158m

COLLAFIRTH

Clubba Water

enclosure. There are extensive ruins of the croft, Ube, ('out by') from whence the last inhabitant, the redoubtable Betty Robertson, would row over to the shop on the other side of Dales Voe. After an hour's walking it is a splendid place to relax and there are some old stone steps to take one down to a delightful small, shingle beach at East Taing. Further along, the beach at West Taing is larger and more exposed. A ruined fishing station stands above it.

Walk round into Dales Voe and on reaching an earth bank, climb up aiming for the fence on top of the hill, the highest point of which is Stouris Nook. On top one has to walk round old peat workings before meeting a well defined cart track. The track goes right along the ridge to a height of 154m and there are great views. There is a wooden gate at a fence and further on a sheep fold where the track, after a dip, starts to rise once more. At Easter Hill of Dale it begins its descent before zigzagging down into Dale.

WALK 17: DALE (DELTING) – SWINISTER

4 miles (6 kms) : 3 hours   If exploring Fora Ness 6 miles (10 kms) : 4 hours

Cycle/Car: Car to Scenic Viewpoint on A970 below Hill of Swinister, cycle to Dale, 4 miles (6 km)

OS Maps: Landranger Sheet 2 Shetland – Whalsay
Explorer 468 Shetland – Mainland North East

If you have hurtled along Dales Lees on the A968 in a car and ever wondered what the shore line of Dales Voe looks like, then this is the walk for you. All this and a chance to explore Fora Ness.

At Dale, start the walk by making for the head of the voe via two metal gates and chest-high cow parsley. Keep well clear of the hay meadows. Reach the mud flats through a wooden gate and take the shingle bar to the west shore. From then on it's a case of boulder bashing along the shore until it gets difficult. Then, climb left and walk on sheep tracks. In the voe observe the latest novelty – shag rafting – and pass a ruined stone enclosure. Cross a burn with a gentle water fall and reach a sea farm jetty. Large eider rafts may be seen and divers, possibly. It's like walking a large lake and from Scarva Ayre the plateau grows and walking becomes easier. Note various

croft ruins, including Southie and Rigg, some with trees are now close and there is a boat noost at the start of a long pebble stretch of foreshore. At the west end of the tombola of South Ayre is a massive square pund with ornate corners, not roofed, but having cobble floors and divided into compartments for sheep and lambs. The walls rise to peaks at the corners to prevent the enclosed sheep from climbing over. It is one of four in Shetland and we shall find another at Garth at Sullom Voe.

Cross the tombola, avoiding the tern colony and explore Fora Ness, as time allows. Hares may be spotted and there are good views from the small cairn on the summit mound.

Return to Swinister can only be made by re-crossing South Ayre – The Houb gets in the way of crossing Swinister Voe by North Ayre. Having re-crossed the ayre, cross a fence and

Haa of Swinister, North Ayre, Swinister Voe.

find what looks like a prehistoric homestead site made up of two circular ruins and further on, a rectangle is made up of large stones for reason unknown. More croft ruins at Oldhall and Northness are now in view, but take time to look at the derelict booth on North Ayre. This, the Haa of Swinister, was once an important store for the locality – today it is the sea farms which are contributing to the Shetland economy.

To end this walk, follow the track up from North Ayre until the Scenic Viewpoint on the A970, below Hill of Swinister, is reached.

Walk 17: DALE (DELTING) – SWINISTER

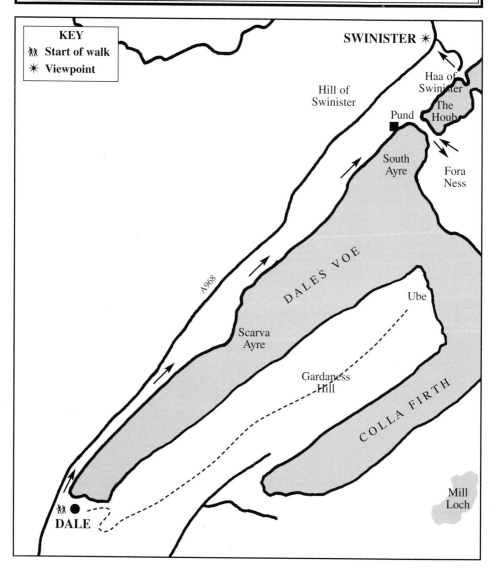

WALK 18: SWINISTER – BROUGH (TOFT)

7 miles (11 kms) : 4 hours

Cycle/Car: Car to Toft Pier, cycle to lay-by on the sharp bend of the A968 at the viewpoint on Hill of Swinister above Firths Voe, 3 miles (5 km). On the junction between the A968 and Mossbank, visit the Delting Disaster Memorial. It is a fitting tribute to the fishermen of Delting who were lost on 21st December, 1900, during a gale.

OS Maps: Landranger Sheet 3 Shetland – North Mainland
Explorer 468 Shetland – Mainland North East

We are now approaching the area where Sullom Voe Terminal construction and subsequent operations have had the most direct impact on the community. Modern housing developments may arouse various reactions but there is much beauty and many sites of interest on this walk which ends at a fine broch site.

From the lay-by go through a metal gate and follow the track down the hill, ignoring the turn left to a BT site. As the track takes a right bend above a ruined croft walk left down a wide green track to another derelict house. Just before the house turn left over a flat area and cross grazing land down to the coastline and a fence, passing corrugated iron sheep shelters. Go through a wooden gate on to lush pasture and note a metal block set in concrete. This is a reminder of the laying of the Ninian oil pipeline as we now cross a section of paved concrete embankment below two Ninian Pipeline triangular signs on poles. At Firth Ness ahead of us is the Isle of Linga, but there is also a good view of the uninhabited Island of Samphrey with a croft house clearly visible. Samphrey has a churchyard reputed not to contain the remains of any men, because they always suffered the fate of death by drowning.

Mossbank lighthouse and Yell come into view. Seals may monitor your progress round into Firths Voe where two gullies can slow one down. At the second gully, climb up stream to cross it near croft ruins and then descend to a gate on the shore line. The sandy beach on the head of the voe is popular with a variety of sea

birds and hidden under the sand, the Brent oil pipeline makes its land fall en route to Sullom Voe. Since it commenced operations in 1978, over 4.6 billion barrels of oil have flowed through it.

Walk through the rank grass below the houses, noting a cairn of large rocks before wading waist high through wild iris leaves to reach the

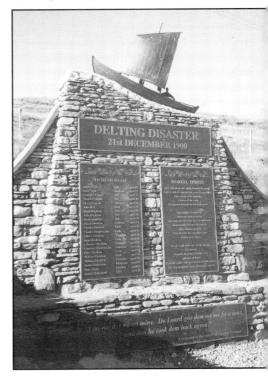

Delting Disaster Memorial, Firth.

71

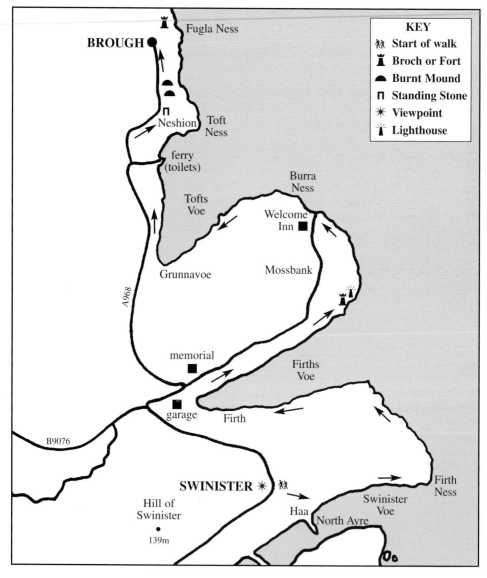

KEY

- 戕 Start of walk
- 🯄 Broch or Fort
- ◖ Burnt Mound
- ⊓ Standing Stone
- ✳ Viewpoint
- 🯅 Lighthouse

BROUGH ●

Fugla Ness

Neshion Toft Ness

ferry (toilets)

Tofts Voe

Burra Ness

Welcome Inn ■

Grunnavoe

Mossbank

A968

memorial ■

Firths Voe

garage ■ Firth

B9076

SWINISTER ✳ 戕

Hill of Swinister

● 139m

Haa North Ayre

Swinister Voe

Firth Ness

lighthouse. This has been constructed in a traditional style on the small promontory of Infield. The 'Inventory' notes that this is also a broch site, beside which a small house, the last occupant of which was affectionately known as "Whippet', has also been erected. It is not obvious today, but evidently the broch diameter of the tower has been approximately 60ft. There are the remains of a chamber and a little further east on the seaward face of the

Two ayres, Swinister Voe and Dales Voe.

Ninian oil pipeline land fall, Firth Ness.

Lighthouse on broch site, Infield, Mossbank.

ruin was a midden where bones, shells and fragments of pottery were found.

A series of plank bridges and stiles helps one reach Mossbank jetty where the magnificently restored and maintained booth vies the Welcome Inn (built 1949, originally with a shop on the ground floor and a knitwear factory upstairs) for attention. The Mossbank church, community hall and primary school will be found further up the road. The ferry from Yell used to depart from here.

At a triangular power cable pole and concrete building where the electricity cable to Yell was originally laid, head right to follow the shore round Grunna Taing and Toft Voe along Burra Ness. Somebody has worked hard in the past to lay a path along the shore line.

Just before reaching the sandy beach at Grunnavoe, note a ring of stones with one large upright on the cliff edge. The beach is popular with people digging the sand in search of razor clams ('spoots') at time of low tides.

Follow the coast round below the main road; some of the cliff bank has been buttressed and by it is a large upright stone. Leave the shore here to climb onto the grass. Walk through some peat banks and pass two small croft ruins. At Toft the booth has sadly been destroyed, but beside a modern bungalow, a water mill ruin still survives. Cross a fence to the pier (Zetland CC Tofts Voe Pier 1951 states a plaque) where there are toilets and a waiting room with telephone.

There is a frequent ferry service from here to Yell, but once, Toft was an important port for Leith traders and whalers. It was here that Dr Richard Pike, a BP engineer at Sullom Voe Terminal, came ashore after swimming Toft Sound from Yell. It took him 2 hours, 9 minutes and 9 seconds on the 24th August, 1980. To date nobody else has followed his example.

Cross the beach and climb onto an area of lush grazing as we aim for Toft Ness. On the slope of the hill between the coast and the road are two burnt mounds midway between Brough and Neshion and a chunky standing stone.

Brough marks the end of this walk but at Fugla Ness near a ruined croft and outbuildings is a most attractive broch site. The entrance to the broch was on the seaward side, where there are still traces of two oval-shaped cells within the thickness of the wall. More obvious are the two ramparts with a wide ditch between them and traces of an outer square outbuilding can be seen. A great place to enjoy some refreshment and look over the waters of Yell Sound.

Standing stone, Toft Ness.

WALK 19: BROUGH (TOFT) – GARTHS VOE

6 miles (10 kms) : 4 hours

Cycle/Car: Car to Garths Voe, cycle to Brough House, 5 miles – (8 km)

OS Maps: Landranger Sheet 3 Shetland – North Mainland
Explorer 468 Shetland – Mainland North East

Easy walking round Mio Ness with its extensive views followed by a stroll round the outside of Sullom Voe Terminal. An attractive optional extra is to climb the Hill of Crooksetter to see two ancient and one modern cairn.

From Brough House at the road end above Toft Pier follow the track between the two bungalows which leads through a wooden and then a metal gate. Aim for the distinctive broch ruin on Fugla Ness before crossing a fence and following the coastline below a croft ruin. There are pebble beaches round Croo Taing and the stone embankment by a small ruin indicates possible use of a fishing station. The uninhabited islands of Bigga, Uynarey and Brother, with attendant islets, dominates the

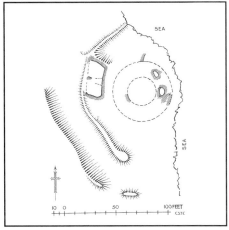

Plan of broch, Fugla Ness, Toft.

Broch, Fugla Ness, Toft.

75

view north east with Yell's west coast as a majestic backdrop.

The lighthouse on Mio Ness has a tripod set in stones beside it and from here are distant views north of the Ramna Stacks, Lamba and Little Roe with its croft ruin on the south end. Ronas and Collafirth hills dominate the north west view.

Soon the oil storage tanks at Sullom Voe come into view. Pass a grassy stack just offshore before walking over ancient peat workings above Aywick. Orka Voe has been filled in with the earth excavated to create the terraces on which the process and storage areas of the terminal are built. Although the gabion sea defences (stone-filled plastic baskets) are outside the terminal security fence, the route to Calback Ness is not an option as there are security gates between Orka Voe and the jetties. All you are missing are some derelict World War II defence positions where it is still possible to walk through the connecting tunnels. A lone pencil drawing of a female nude, with her hair in the style of Rita Hayworth, brightens up the concrete walls of one of the dug-outs. So, climb up to a large

Walk 19: BROUGH (TOFT) – GARTHS VOE

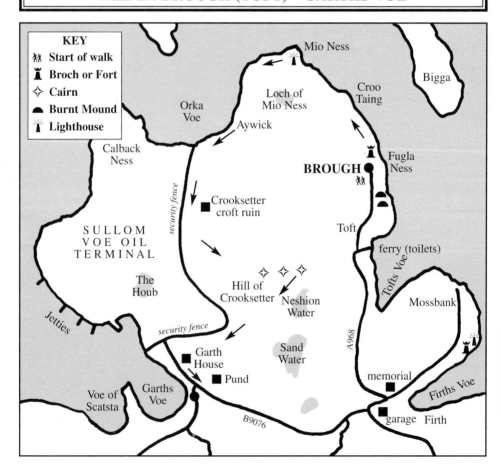

Croft at Crooksetter, Sullom Voe Terminal.

croft ruin (if the last crofter could come back he would wonder where the sea has gone) and climb up the Hill of Crooksetter (378ft). From the two chambered cairns on the hill summit are extensive views. One cairn has been much disturbed and the stones piled up; the other is rather more overgrown. A little further on is a cairn with small sections of the Brent and Ninian pipelines joined to form a cross. A plaque on the plinth states,

To
The People of Shetland
From
**The Workforce at
Sullom Voe
21 June 1981**

It was erected in September 1981 to commemorate the construction of Sullom Voe Terminal. The Head Teacher of Brae School, George Peterson said, "So much in the modern world is evidence of man's greed and indifference. Here we have a splendid symbol of man's co-operation and care for one another."

From here descend towards the main flare and follow the outside of the security fence back down to the main road. The prominent house to the east of the road is the restored Garth House. A large square sheep pund was built to its south east in Victorian times. If you have parked in the car park between the terminal and the Seamen's Mission you will find a memorial plaque to Royal Air Force Station,

Chambered cairn, Hill of Crooksetter.

Construction workforce memorial, Hill of Crooksetter, Sullom Voe Terminal.

Roll on my posting slip
This place gives me the pip
Roll on the posting slip of mine
Some day I know I'll go
Far away from Sullom Voe
And leave the bloomin' Shetland far behind

No more peat, squelch
No more suffering from gum boot feet
No more sheep, baa
Every time I see a sheep
It makes me want to weep

The flying boat crews flew many missions requiring great endurance with both RAF and Norwegian aircraft, mainly Sunderland and Catalina, tasked with combat and convoy escort patrols. 210 Squadron carried out highly secret operations including a flight over the North Pole. The 'Arctic Airmen' made flights frequently over 24 hours in length in conditions of great cold.

On 17th July, 1944, Flt Lt John ('Jock') Cruickshank, Captain of Catalina flying boat JV928 of 210 Squadron, whilst on patrol attacked and sank U-boat 347. During the attack Flt Lt Cruickshank was severely wounded but succeeded in returning his badly damaged aircraft safely back to Sullom Voe. For his actions throughout the patrol Flt Lt Cruickshank was awarded the Victoria Cross. Today, John Cruickshank VC lives in Aberdeen and is President of 210 Squadron Association.

RAF memorial, 'Rangatiri' car park, Sullom Voe Oil Terminal.

Sullom Voe and a graphic illustration of what functions the station carried out. The car park used to be known as the 'Rangatiri' car park, for the accommodation ship of this name was berthed here during the terminal construction period.

The attractions of this area were often lost on RAF personnel stationed here during World War II. A song was composed, an extract of the words of which are:

WALK 20: GARTHS VOE – MAVIS GRIND ▮▮▮▮▮▮▮▮

10 miles (16 kms) : 5 hours

Cycle/Car: Car to Mavis Grind, cycle to Garths Voe, 7 miles – (11 km)

OS Maps: Landranger Sheet 3 Shetland – North Mainland
Explorer 468 Shetland – Mainland North East

A superb walk to complete the Eastside Way. The terrain is excellent with only one scramble to climb round Voxter Voe. Otherwise, enjoy extensive views across Sullom Voe, Shetland's largest voe, where the impact of tankers at the jetties and aircraft in and out of Scatsta is surprisingly little considering the importance of the operations.

The cycle ride from Mavis Grind takes one along the A970 to Brae and then the B9076 north east to Garths Voe. The Burn of Valayre and Loch of Trondavoe (red throated divers in summer, occasionally whooper swans in winter) are particularly attractive. On the east of the road opposite Scatsta Airfield runway is Frank Hunter's Scatsta Farm beside which is the old Scatsta Church building dedicated to St Paul. During the war a Spitfire was painted on one of the walls, but has now deteriorated and gone. Scatsta Airfield was built for RAF Scatsta and completed in 1941 to provide fighter cover facilities for RAF Sullom Voe. It also provided a satellite airfield to Shetland's only other war-time RAF airfield at Sumburgh. After war-time service, it was re-opened to support Sullom Voe Terminal operations in 1978 and is still doing that and now, additionally, offshore oil personnel movements.

Above Graven is the site of a medieval church (St Magnus), the well kept cemetery at Loxobigging and the RAF Sullom Voe Camp cinema/theatre, where artists, including Vera Lyn, are reputed to have entertained the troops. I once received a letter from somebody who camped beside Garths Voe in 1958. Christopher Burton wrote:

It was so quiet that on one still Sunday morning, when I was out on the Voe in my canoe, *'Scorie', not far from Ungam, I could hear the congregation in Sullom kirk singing a metrical psalm.*

Those were the days! We camped near the slipway, collected our drinking water from the old RAF tap and cooked the mackerel that we caught from the canoe over a driftwood fire.

From Garths Voe head south west along the road to pass a plantation of bushes and trees opposite the telephone exchange and the war-time fuel bunkers refurbished to play a role today. A road heads down to Sella Ness where the Shetland Islands Council Port Control pilot boats, the Shetland Towage tugs and the terminal pollution control vessels and base are located.

The Houb of Scatsta is a protected salt marsh site with its own oil spill boom facility. In a lay-by see a Sullom Voe Terminal commemorative plaque on a stone base. It

A wartime painting of a Spitfire at Scatsta Kirk.
© Terry Mayes

combines information with a celebration of the 5 billionth barrel of oil being exported from the terminal on 23rd December, 1993. The terminal has now processed over 7.2 billion barrels of oil.

On 13th November, 1939, the Second World War's first air raid on Britain took place here. The first bombing run was aimed at flying boats moored in the voe, but the bombs fell into the deep peat of Sella Ness and failed to explode. The second run saw four bombs fall on the unoccupied croft at Houll and finally, the bomber jettisoned the remaining four bombs above Brae. The BBC announced that the only casualty was a rabbit and this led to

Walk 20: GARTHS VOE – MAVIS GRIND

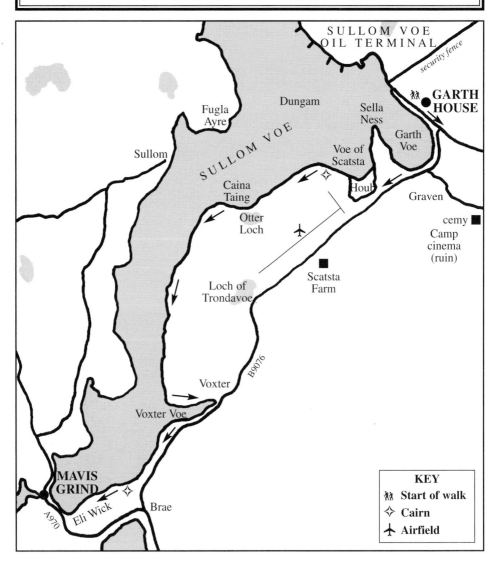

SULLOM VOE OIL TERMINAL

security fence

GARTH HOUSE

Dungam

Fugla Ayre

Sella Ness

Garth Voe

Sullom

SULLOM VOE

Voe of Scatsta

Houll

Graven

Caina Taing

cemy

Camp cinema (ruin)

Otter Loch

Scatsta Farm

Loch of Trondavoe

B9076

Voxter

Voxter Voe

MAVIS GRIND

Eli Wick

Brae

A970

KEY
🚶 **Start of walk**
✧ **Cairn**
✈ **Airfield**

Sullom Voe Oil Terminal commemorative plaque, Houb of Scatsta.

Sullom Voe from Grona Taing.

Taking a break at Voxter House.

many cartoons in both the German and British newspapers. Pictures of a dead rabbit in the seven foot bomb crater at Sullom also appeared – after a Lerwick photographer had obtained one from a butcher's shop and positioned it there.

A clothes-iron stand made from a fragment of the first bomb to fall can be seen today at Gardiesting, Mid Yell, the home of Elizabeth Morewood to whom it was bequeathed by her Aunt Annie.

Leave the road to go through a metal gate. Walk along Houb of Scatsta and after passing a boom site, note a raised and kerbed cairn on the shore of Voe of Scatsta. It measures 33ft in diameter and some stones mark the line of a passage leading into a chamber. Many stones were moved to build a bridge over the nearby North Burn. There are good views from here of the terminal and any tankers loading. One hundred yards further on is a square cairn made up of large stones.

It is easy going round Scatsta Ness and eventually we meet the western end of the war-time runway. I first knew the area when the American Coastguard had a Loran Station here.

The original maintenance force at the terminal worked for Sullom Voe Engineers and staff were largely recruited in South Wales. They were accommodated also in this area in their own village, known as 'Happy Valley'. Today

it is an area for drying commercial peat cuttings.

Pass another small cairn just before the wide sandy beach with its own boom site at Houbs Ayre. Otter Loch is right on the coastline and water from it flows fast to the sea. Across Sullom Voe stands a large jetty, a plantation of trees north above some houses and Sullom kirk.

At Caina Taing climb up into the hill and survey the antics of seals who may abandon lie ups on Bio Wick to monitor your progress. Cross a gully with its dashing burn, watch out for herons and go round a rocky knoll. The houses of Brae come into view as we pass a sheep fold and a cairn above a beach. The next gully has no burn but has been affected by a landslip which requires care to cross.

Voxter Voe has boom sites to allow chevron shaped booms to link to a buoy and so, seal the voe. Pass a small stone ruin and then scramble up, around and down a bluff of cliff. Take great care here and slide down if necessary!

Voxter House is now in view as we descend to pass four boat noosts and two winches, one of which is in excellent condition. Above Voxter House is a very large tree plantation and in front of the house (the former manse of Delting church, the parish church at Scatsta) is a walled garden with trees and a picnic area. The house also saw service as a military hospital in World War II. Jack Manuell, a Cornishman who served on Calback Ness with the Royal Artillery in 1941, met his wife, Alice, at the hospital and has lived in Yell ever since. I asked him what conditions were like on Calback Ness. "It was terrible," he recalled. "We had two four-inch naval guns and two searchlights. We were completely cut-off and there was virtually nothing to do. Most of the men were Cockneys and they couldn't believe such a place could exist. Apart from occasionally guiding in damaged Sunderlands, by using our searchlights, all we did was spend days gathering shingle in sandbags to make paths." Jack returned to Calback Ness forty years later in 1981 to work for Sullom Voe

Engineers. "Of my two experiences of working in Calback Ness, give me the construction days of Sullom Voe Terminal any time," Jack smiled. "They were proper job!"

Leave the picnic area by crossing a stile and salt marsh to climb up towards the road and follow it safely inside the wire fence by using sheep tracks. At Scarva Taing descend to the beach leaving it to climb up to lush grazing land with a ruin of a concrete block building near Northbrae. A wooden gate in a fence is reached and shortly afterwards, note a prehistoric cairn 100yds up from the shore line. Leave the grazing land to descend to Eli Wick, the extreme south point of Sullom Voe and cross the shingle beach to reach the main road. Turn right up the road, passing a former quarry area and reach the sign indicating Mavis Grind.

The Eastside Way ends here, but it is the start point for the North Mainland Trek and the Westside Way. Think on!

Journey's end, Mavis Grind.

Ro-Ro ferry usually from Laxo but under certain weather conditions from Vidlin in which case there is a roadside indicator. Regular 30 minute crossing bookable by telephoning Symbister (01806) 566259. Loganair flights from Tingwall may be available on request.

OS Maps: **Landranger Sheet 2 Shetland – Whalsay**
Explorer 468 Shetland – Mainland North East

Whalsay, the 'bonnie isle', offers a great deal to the walker. It may not have the dramatic scenery to be found on some other Shetland islands, but it is sufficiently hilly to make it both an attractive place to walk and from which to view the many islands and stacks around it.

Whalsay is five and a half miles (8km) long and two miles (3km) at its broadest. The fishing industry in Whalsay is the main support for a population of about 1000 people, with the main settlement being at Symbister. Here is a protected harbour large enough to accommodate the Whalsay fishing fleet and fish processing plant. During the Napoleonic Wars, reports Dr Robert Cowie, the burning of seaweed for kelp employed many Whalsay women, but it soon became uneconomic.

The ferry route takes one through Dury Voe between the coastlines of North Nesting and Lunnasting. Small islands are dotted along the route, but it is the large uninhabited island of West Linga and its Calf which lie nearest to Whalsay.

Dominating the steep east hill of Symbister stands Symbister House. This was built by Bruce of Symbister from Nesting granite at a cost of £30,000 in 1823. Since the 1960s the house has been the local school, but behind it

is the midden yard with its belfry and dove cot and other buildings which will benefit from the involvement of the Whalsay History Group.

On landing make a visit to a 17th century stone pier house used by Bremen merchants as a Hanseatic Bod which was restored and opened to the public in 1984.

Whalsay also boasts the excellent Symbister Leisure Centre, which includes a swimming pool, Whalsay Golf Club on the north point of the island and many features worth exploring on foot. These include prehistoric archaeological sites, brochs and forts, the many lochs and a coastline with a variety of birdlife.

This book describes walks which take one round Whalsay in two days. Self-catering accommodation is offered by:

- Oot-Ower Lounge at Livister with meals (booking essential) (01806) 566658
- The Grieve House Camping Bod, Sodom (01595) 693434 and;
- 1 Bothies, Symbister, (01806) 566429.

Stores may be purchased at Tetley & Anderson, general grocer, off-sales, in-store bakery, butchers and post office (01806) 566585/566601.

CIRCULAR WALK A

WHALSAY – SOUTH CIRCULAR
Symbister – Sandwick – Hevda – Loch of Huxter – Ward of Clett – Symbister
7 miles (11 km) : 4 hours

No difficult terrain on this interesting walk round the southern coastline of Whalsay. One real climb, from the fort on Loch of Huxter to the top of Ward of Clett with its splendid views.

From the ferry terminal explore the main harbour where some of Shetland's largest fishing boats, with names like *Serene*, *Research*, *Charisma* and *Zephyr* may be seen. The marina in the inner harbour provides berths for rowing boats and sailing dinghies.

Walk past the fish processing factory and climb over a fence to walk along a track to

Symbister Harbour, Whalsay.

Chambered cairn, Symbister Ness, Whalsay.

Burnt mound, Loch of Sandwick, Whalsay.

pass to the right of a quarry. The square panels of the lighthouse on Bruga are not as photogenic as a traditional light. Pass a power cable landfall sign and take in the views up Dury Voe, with the Whalsay ferries passing each other and south west, to Hog Island, Noss and Bressay. Symbister Ness boasts a chambered cairn at its high point on the Ward. It is made up of fairly large stones and may originally have been pear shaped, 45ft by 35ft and at least 3ft 6ins high. Go round the Point of Gruid where the geos sparkle and are pleasing to view and note a large otter trap built with large stones and a stretch of wall built as a weather protection for sheep. In

Circular Walk A: WHALSAY – SOUTH CIRCULAR

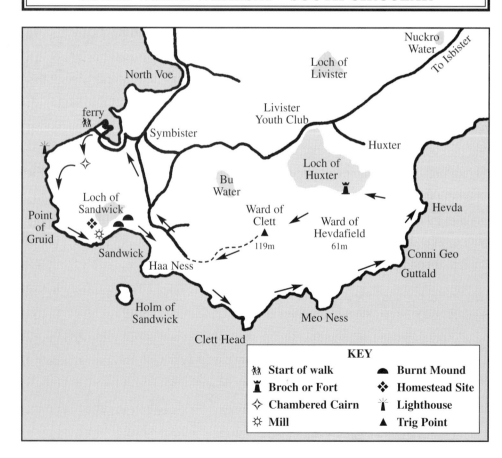

Nuckro Water
To Isbister
Loch of Livister
North Voe
ferry
Livister Youth Club
Symbister
Huxter
Loch of Huxter
Bu Water
Loch of Sandwick
Ward of Clett
Hevda
Point of Gruid
Ward of Hevdafield
61m
△ 119m
Sandwick
Conni Geo
Haa Ness
Guttald
Holm of Sandwick
Meo Ness
Clett Head

KEY

𝅘 Start of walk		⬣ Burnt Mound
♜ Broch or Fort		❖ Homestead Site
◇ Chambered Cairn		🕯 Lighthouse
☼ Mill		▲ Trig Point

Otter trap, near Point of Gruid.

1942, an RAF Sullom Voe Catalina flying boat made an emergency landing and came ashore here. All the crew were saved.

To the north, Symbister House comes into view whilst in the cliffs a cave can be spotted and a dramatic red natural arch. Make your way through a large stone wall by using an excellent wooden stile. There are often ducks on the Loch of Sandwick and along its shore stand five planticrubs. At least one water mill was once powered by the burn running from the loch to a shingle beach on the shore.

At a stone ruin of a sheep fold cross a stile and climb the mound where stands a solitary stone cairn and descend towards the loch, passing the stone ruins of four prehistoric houses in a field system. There are two burnt mounds, one on the south margin of the loch and the other, 100 yards south east of it.

Now make for Sandwick Bay through a metal gate and note a winch before crossing the bay to use a stile to access the banks. There is quite

a rocky scramble to reach Haa Ness where there is a stone enclosure ruin opposite Holm of Sandwick. A stile helps one round a geo and in an area of grazing land four stone clearance cairns will be seen. Climb up to a gate by a high wire mesh fence at the geo, formerly used as the island tip.

Go through two metal gates to gain access to open country and at Clett Head note an offshore rock which resembles a submarine. Climb over a block stile to descend the slope to the peaceful valley of Braewick. Cross the burn to round Meo Ness with its sheep fold. Above a small shingle beach, previous visitors have created a bench and table from driftwood. Another block stile takes one over a wire fence to a high open stone enclosure facing south west on a bluff of land.

At Guttald is a cairn with six upright stones and from here, climb over the Ward Hevdafield (61m) where a well defined track goes past a croft ruin to the many stone cairns on its summit. At Hevda we are almost opposite,

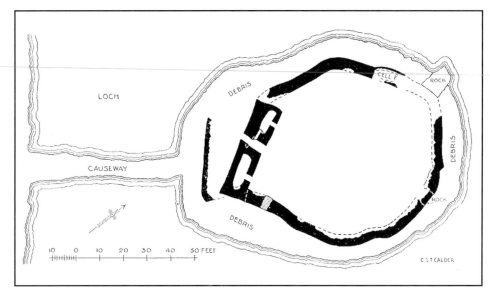

Plan of fort, Loch of Huxter, Whalsay.

Fort, Loch of Huxter, Whalsay.

Trig Point, Ward of Clett, Whalsay

east, the islets of East Linga and Grif Skerry. Here, in 1750, the Russian frigate *Isslaffa* was wrecked and most of the crew lost. However, the Whalsay men saved some of the crew and a letter of thanks was sent by the Empress Catherine of Russia.

From Hevda leave the coast to head west to Loch of Huxter and seek out the ruin of a blockhouse fort built on a small island lying off the south shore. Connection with the shore was by a roughly built causeway 64ft long and from 6ft to 12ft wide. The interior of the fort itself is roughly circular and about 70ft in diameter. The fort has been robbed of much stone which has been recycled as four planticrubs nearby and the former school at Livister.

From the Loch of Huxter climb the Ward of Clett where stand the ruins of an RAF World

War II radar site, part of the Home Chain Radar System which covered the whole of the UK. Clett was one of the radar sites which covered Shetland and was the most northerly site in the UK (the other two were at Watts Ness in Walls and at Sumburgh).

There are large areas of hard standing and two brick block houses beside the Trig Point (119m, 393ft) from which are superb views, not only distant panoramas, but also of Symbister and the several planticrubs near the Loch of Bin Water.

From the ward follow the crumbling military road down the hill to return to Symbister. The route takes one past some lovely houses. There is a great pride shown in many of the gardens, with that of 'Finjari' being particularly memorable, all living up to the reputation that Whalsay is indeed 'Da Bonnie Isle'.

WHALSAY – NORTH CIRCULAR
Symbister – Isbister – Skaw – Symbister

12 miles (19 km) : 6 hours

or

Isbister – Skaw – Symbister

8 miles (13 km) : 4 hours

Cycle/Car:	No car necessary for the long walk. Cycle or get a lift to Isbister for the shorter walk.
OS Maps:	Landranger Sheet 2 Shetland – Whalsay Explorer 468 Shetland – Mainland North East

A long walk on easy terrain which presents no difficulties for the walker, though a strong north east wind would slow one down. A walk rich in prehistoric remains, some fine scenery and bird life, particularly in late May or early June when there is often a late passage of migrants.

From the ferry terminal climb up through Symbister to take the road to Isbister. At Sodom, north of the road is The Grieve House, the home of Hugh MacDiarmid, the celebrated Scots poet, between 1933 and 1942 and today a Camping Bod.

As the road rounds the north shore of Loch of Huxter is Oot Ower Lounge. If taking the road to Isbister, then beware of phantoms at the next

Thatched byre near Isbister, Whalsay.

loch, Nuckro Water. This loch is named after the 'nykr', a horse-like phantom which dragged people to death by drowning in the loch. It is also reputed to be an area where trows are active at night-time.

To walk the coastal route, head east from Loch of Huxter to join the banks at Hevda and walk north past Veeda Stack and Poier Head. Just in land is the now abandoned township of Treawick; evidently the people did not want a road and eventually the area was deserted. Note the large stone walls near the shore before climbing up from Colvigirts, past a former ship's lifeboat boathouse to reach

Boat shed near Isbister.

Circular Walk B: WHALSAY – NORTH CIRCULAR

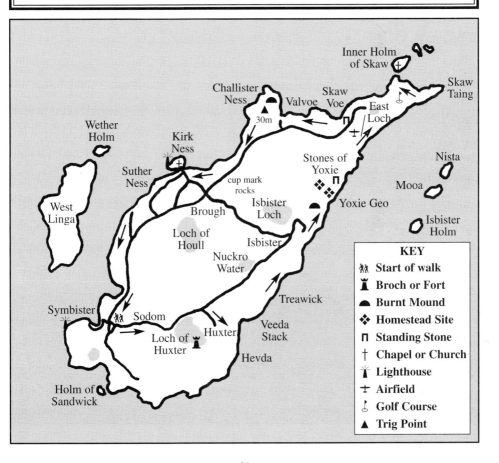

Isbister. Use the wooden stile when a high tensile and barb wire fence is encountered.

Isbister is a popular place to live and the thriving population enjoy a reasonably sheltered location beside a loch. The sites of two burnt mounds have been identified. The coast can be reached by a grassy track and the next natural feature is Longi Geo. Walk on to Yoxie Geo where there is a prehistoric homestead site above the shore line, known as the "Stones of Yoxie". Inland, 300 yards up the slope is the excavated prehistoric farmhouse site known as "The Benie Hoose". A highlight of this walk is to explore the stones of this remarkable Neolithic survivor once thought to have been a temple. To the west further up Gamla Vord there is a heel-shaped cairn on the shoulder of the hill. It is now a mass of tumbled stones, but its chamber and passage were once paved and from it are good views of the Mainland as well as the islands closer to Whalsay. Some islets are quite close to the shore as we head past Whelsiego Stacks and approach the strikingly green fairway of the golf course. A convenient bridge takes us over a geo, but a bench on the hill might delay us. Pass the southern end of the airstrip and East Loch of Skaw, with a burnt mound on the west shore, to climb up to the cairn on Skaw Taing. Head round the bay, passing two planticrubs and a power cable sign by a shingle beach. Off Sponger Point are Outer Holm and Inner Holm of Skaw, the latter having the ruins of a medieval or earlier chapel on it.

The next stretch of coastline is remarkable for its collection of geos, gates and boat winches. Sheep get a nose in for we also pass a sheep fold. A former flit boat converted into a shed in 1955 with windows is now decayed, but other boats are berthed on the beaches. Skaw Voe boasts four winches and a standing stone known locally as, "The Stone of the Toon". It

Prehistoric farmhouse site, Yoxie. Nista and Mooa islands beyond.

Standing stone and horse, near Valvoe, Skaw Voe.

Robbie Simpson and *Violet*.

stands about 50 yards from the shore, 4ft 9ins high, 8ft 6ins in girth, the survivor of possibly three standing stones in this area. It was guarded by a fine horse.

At Valvoe a harbour has been created and mussel rafts established. Here lives Robbie Simpson, a former colleague of mine at Sullom Voe Terminal. He was restoring a foureen originally built in 1887 called *Violet* and once used for fishing haddock. Robbie has also restored an even older sixereen named *Gleaning* which he had taken to Lerwick with a square sail for the 'Tall Ships Race' gathering.

Follow the coast round to Challister Ness which boasts a Trig Point (30m) on the ward and a burnt mound at Oo Knowe north of the township.

We now walk on to Kirkness which is well worth spending time on. The church and medieval chapel site, dedicated to Holy Rood and burial ground are certainly in a beautiful

location. Here also are the war memorials for the people of Whalsay who lost their lives in World Wars I and II. There are tern colonies on the shingle beach and a modern lighthouse on Suther Ness.

As we walk on, Brough Head is a reminder of the broch which the 'Inventory' places on the

Cup markings, Brough, Whalsay.

top of a hill near the church, although no definite remains are visible. At Brough, bronze Age "cup marks" have been pecked out (not ground) of the exposed surfaces of living rock (as opposed to detached stones). In all they total about 40 bowl shaped cavities and the OS map marks two sites, near Cready Knowe and towards The Houb. Many theories have been put forward to try and explain "cup marks" (and "ring marks" of which there are none here). Theories range from boundary markers to signifying sites of religious and magical significance. As yet, there is no evidence to support any theory.

The island of West Linga now dominates the view west as we walk past Marrister with its navigation light in Linga Sound and a salmon farm. North Point leads in to North Voe and the care centre for Whalsay before our, no doubt, welcome descent back to Symbister ferry terminal.

Kirk Ness, Whalsay.

CIRCULAR WALK C

OUT SKERRIES
Ferry Terminal Bruray – Housay – Bruray

7 miles (11 km) : 4 hours

OS Maps: **Landranger Sheet 2 Shetland – Whalsay**
Explorer 468 Shetland – Mainland North East

Out Skerries (known as 'Skerries') hold many attractions for the walker and a visit to the islands combines a memorable ferry journey with pleasant walking on easy terrain. The two inhabited main islands are Bruray, which has the ferry terminal and airstrip and Housay which is joined to it by a bridge built in 1957. On the uninhabited island of Grunay are the former houses of the lighthouse keepers who manned the light on Bound Skerry. The

Circular Walk C: OUT SKERRIES

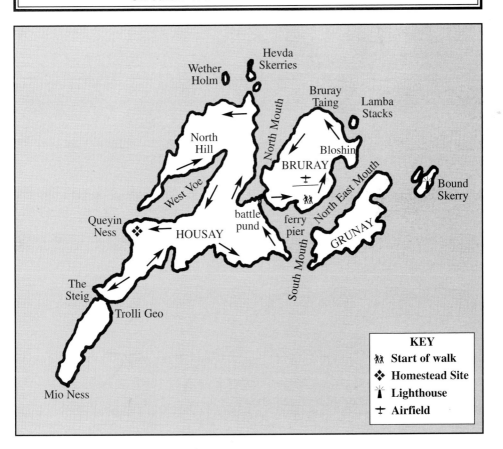

KEY
ᴀ Start of walk
❖ Homestead Site
☀ Lighthouse
✝ Airfield

View of the South Mouth, Out Skerries.

lighthouse was erected (like the Unst and Bressay lighthouses) by Messrs D & T Stevenson in 1852 and rises to a height of 96ft.

The islands are grouped round a superb natural harbour – an ideal base for fishing boats and hence a population of nearly a hundred people. There is no peat on Skerries, but there is a band of limestone which supports fertile grazing land. Bird-watchers visit Skerries, particularly, to spot what is often the first land fall for migrant birds blown off course by south

Trying and failing to cross The Steig, Out Skerries.

westerly gales. I will never forget drawing the curtains in a self-catering chalet to see on otter looking up enquiringly.

The active community living in Skerries supports a school, church, shop, village hall, post office, fish factory and fishing boats and salmon farming. A great place to stay and explore. Loganair flights (01595) 840248 or ferry bookings (01806) 515226 will get you there.

Start the walk at the ferry terminal and head up the road turning right past a telephone box to the coastline of the North East Mouth. Pass the end of the airstrip and make for Head of Bloshin and a view of inshore Lamba Stack. Note a natural arch between here and dramatic Bruray Taing. Make your way down North Mouth to cross Skerries Bridge to Housay. Follow the road leaving it before the cemetery to walk up the west coast of North Mouth and gain height by climbing up North Ward (40m) and North Hill (43m) with its row of planticrubs. Aim for the east coast of West Voe and walk on to Queyin Ness which has a great mass of rocky outcrops and boulders round which the waves can foam. There are two Neolithic house sites on this ness. Mio Ness is virtually an island with an inlet, Trolli Geo and a rift, 90yds long, known as The Steig. I have only tried to make it once, on hands and knees up the precipitous, sloping, slippery, rocky shelf and would not recommend the experience. The Ward of Mioness (48m) can be seen from afar and our route heads back to South Mouth where, behind some houses is a stone rectangle known as the Skerries Battle Pund. Here, it is thought armed men, possibly chained together, fought out their disputes to a bloody conclusion.

Another such pund is associated with Little Holm lying west off Scat Ness, Sumburgh. A well recorded 'Skerry Fight' involved the Gifford family in a clash with a female-led party of Sinclairs. The argument centred on the summer use of temporary fishing huts and booths. The Gifford family took armed possession of the huts and when Magnus Flaws of the Sinclair band tried to access a booth through the roof, he was shot dead. "Upon which the Sinclairs took flight, and, like dastards, abandoned their lady, who was by the opposite party made prisoner," reported Samuel Hibbert.

From the battle pund cross back over the bridge and return to the ferry terminal to complete this walk.

Bed & Breakfast is available at Rocklea. (01806) 515228.

BRESSAY

RoRo ferry from Lerwick . Regular 5 minute crossing, not bookable.

OS Maps: **Landranger Sheet 4 Shetland – South Mainland**
                 Explorer 467 Shetland – Mainland Central
                 Explorer 466 Shetland – Mainland South

Bressay is a wonderful island to explore on foot; it is full of interest and some splendid scenery.

As far as distances are concerned, Bressay is bigger than it looks. It may only measure 7 x 3 miles, (11 x 8 km) but to walk it and enjoy it requires three or four days. Advantage should also be taken of visiting Noss from Bressay and Noss, itself, can be a three hour walk.

The most dramatic cliff scenery is in the south of the island and some of it can only be fully appreciated from a boat. Dr Jonathan Wills lives on Bressay and operates Seabirds-and-Seals from Lerwick. So, contact him for cruises round Bressay to Noss (Tel: 01595 693434) and enjoy memorable views from the sea.

Up to about 1800 most people lived on the east side of Bressay and the north east quarter of the island is particularly rich in historical features. For this reason, if you only have time for one walk on Bressay, then the track round Aith Ness to Setter would be my recommendation. However, the wide ranging views from Ward of Bressay (226m) are worth the climb and from the peak you can even gaze down speculatively on Muckle Hell.

It is an island of big guns. There is still an enormous naval gun on the cliffs of the Bard at the south end of the island and another on Aith Ness on the north coast.

The Shetland Member of the Scottish Parliament, (MSP) Tavish Scott and the Lord Lieutenant of Shetland, John Scott are both residents of Bressay, as is the poet, Stella Sutherland.

Accommodation is limited on Bressay and not available on Noss. On Bressay the Maryfield House Hotel near the ferry terminal offers a warm welcome and good quality home cooking in a family run hotel. (01595) 820207.

Ovluss, natural arch, Kirkabister Ness, Bressay.

CIRCULAR WALK D

BRESSAY – SOUTH CIRCULAR
Kirkabister Ness – Kirkabister – Ward of Bressay – Grutwick – Green Head – Bard Head – Kirkabister Ness

7 miles (11 km) : 4 hours

Cycle/Car: Car or cycle to Kirkabister, 3 miles (5 km)

OS Maps: Landranger Sheet 4 Shetland – South Mainland
                     Explorer 466 Shetland – Mainland South

The start point at the lighthouse is a three mile walk from the ferry terminal near the Maryfield Hotel, so a car or bicycle would be useful. Otherwise, add six miles to the distance shown. It is a walk which can give a great deal of pleasure and the challenges of climbing the Ward and the Mills of the Ord. The gun on the Bard awaits inspection but keep clear of the gantry – it is right on the cliff edge!

Start the walk from the lighthouse, now automatic, which was built in 1858 by the Stevenson brothers. From here, walk the road north up the hill to the collection of dwellings at Kirkabister. Behind the croft up the slope to the south is the site of St John's Chapel and burial ground; it may be seen by a wire fence where a hill track was built.

Possible monastic site opposite Stoura Clett, Bressay. Noss beyond.

Now head north east up the slopes of Ward Hill which is dominated by television masts – Shetland's first mast was erected here by the BBC in 1964. At the top, a small circular cairn with a wooden floor is built round the Trig Point, 742ft (226m). Recover from the climb here by enjoying extensive views before heading east for Grutwick. Take care, there are

Circular Walk D: BRESSAY – SOUTH CIRCULAR

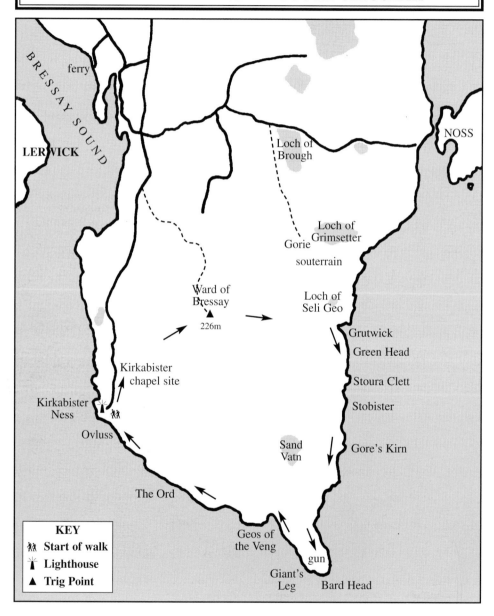

green 'sinky places'. Noss provides a dramatic backdrop to this descent.

Grutwick beach has boulders all the time and seals occasionally. From here head south down the coast, enjoying Green Head and the triple arch of Stoura Clett Stack. Worth visiting, though great care is needed, is the ancient site built high up on a shelf on the cliff face just north of the islet of Stoura Clett. When this stack becomes fully visible on the climb up the hill following the wire fence, climb over the fence and look down on the substantial shelf below. Descend with care to the remains of two dry stone buildings lying within 50 yards of each other. They contain stone cupboard/shelves in irregular-shaped cells. Originally, this could have been a Celtic monastic cell site, because it is just the sort of place the monks would have looked for. As the site is so difficult to find, it may, also, have been used by people seeking to escape the press-gang during the Napoleonic Wars. Further south along the cliff face is the remains of a dry stone building. It marks the ancient settlement site of Stobister. According to legend, one of the reasons people abandoned the site was the result of a particularly rough winter gale, when fish were thrown out of the sea and down the chimneys of the houses!

The cliffs are often precipitous with an almost perpendicular fall of 80ft to the sea below, so care is needed when trying to spot Gore's Kirn, a collapsed sea cave and the Hole of Burgars. Near to the cliff are derelict slate quarries worked in the 1790s. Virtually on the cliff edge is a huge boulder called, "The Kirning Stone of the Gore's Kirn".

Pass a sheep pund and another cairn and notice the gun gantry come into view. Climb up past a cairn with a small standing stone in a quarry area and make for the gun. This six-inch naval gun was raised on 3rd April, 1918 to guard the southern approaches. It is a more risky site to explore than the gun site on Aith Ness because the cliffs are sheer. The gantry is right on the cliff edge and it can be very windy here. Shelter can be enjoyed in the bunker behind the gun, but lower your head when entering it.

Possible monastic site opposite Stoura Clett, Bressay.

Laurence Anderson maintains a Visitors Book on behalf of the community and there is a pen for you to enter your name in it.

Below, but not visible from the cliff top is the natural arch, Giant's Leg, through which a boat can pass and the Cave of the Bard, also known as The Orkney Man's Cave. Here an Orcadian

The Giant's Leg with a boat towing a barge which carried the two six inch guns for the Head of the Bard and Elvis Voe.   © Shetland Museum

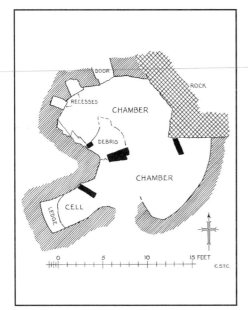

Stoura Clett structures.

fled from the press-gang, whilst above, a local crofter, Jeemie Lamb, made his escape from the gang by hiding on a grassy ledge below the overhanging east face of the Bard.

Descend to the Geos of the Veng ("the caves below the meadow") and enjoy a delightful spot. Seals lie up on slabs of rock and water cascades from above. Mill Burn also tumbles down from the loch of Sand Vatn and the Burn of Veng to make the area a remarkable area of waterfalls.

Cross the stone bridge before climbing to a large stone enclosure within which another enclosure shelters a steel storage tank. Pass through a wooden gate by a sheep fold and take a well marked track up the Mills of Ord to the high and precipitous Cliff of the Ord. Near the top a wire fence stops sheep from falling over the edge. The cliff top has several fissures where the ground has eroded, so keep well in. Soon the lighthouse comes into view below at

Cairn, Loch of Seligeo, Bressay. Bard Head beyond.

102

South gun, Head of the Bard, Bressay. Noss beyond.

Kirkabister Ness, a sight made all the more impressive by the view of the natural arch named Ovluss. Follow a wire fence down to a metal gate to the right of which is a stile and walk through the ruined crofts of Serana and Daal to the road.

If you are walking back to Maryfield or the ferry terminal you can take the road diverting to the shore line to, for example, one of the several sites for former herring curing stations, Taing of Ham. Today it is an area where tussock grass grows.

At Grindiscol about 100yds north and about midway between the road and the shore is a burnt mound. It measured 54ft in diameter and 7ft 6ins in height. When excavated it revealed large stones at the bottom, one of which was erect and appeared to have a passage leading to it.

The road goes through areas of modern housing and passes the church, Mail Shop, Post Office, School, Public Hall and Marina. Across the Voe of Leiraness the rocky Holme of the Ness was a broch site, now demolished.

The ferry terminal commissioned for the first inter-island vehicle ferry in 1975, is now but a short stroll away. Today the ferry is fittingly called *Leirna*.

South naval gun bunker entrance, Head of the Bard.

CIRCULAR WALK E ∎

BRESSAY – NORTH CIRCULAR
Maryfield Ferry Terminal – Heogan – Aith Ness – Cullingsburgh – Maryfield

14 miles (23 km) : 7 hours

OS Maps: Landranger Sheet 4 Shetland – South Mainland
                Explorer 467 Shetland – Mainland Central

A long walk, but one not requiring transport on the island. A shortened version featuring Aith Ness will be found at Circular Walk G.

The walk includes a notable standing stone, two medieval chapel sites, a giant naval gun and the quarries, which provided much of the Lerwick building stone.

Standing stone, Hill of Cruester, Bressay.

From the ferry walk up to the car park where the Bressay Heritage Centre (01595 820750) may be visited. The Centre displays items of local history and outside lies the anchor used to hold down the wartime defence boom across the harbour.

At Maryfield House Hotel turn left and walk the road to Heogan. On the left stands the impressive Gardie House, built in 1724 from local sandstone and currently, the home of the Lord Lieutenant of Shetland. Above the fireplace in the hall is a stone panel from the old, now roofless, farmhouse of Garth dating back to 1579.

Further along the shore line is a burnt mound, but of more note is the standing stone in a prominent position on the Hill of Cruester, north of Gardie House and reached across pasture land. It is 9ft 6in high and 4ft 6in wide at the base and has now a decided tilt to SSW. Return to the Heogan road, noting the ruins of wartime gun emplacements and descend to the large fish-meal factory operated by Shetland Fish Products Ltd. and providing local employment. There used to be a broch site beyond the factory, but it was demolished when a fishing station was established here in the 18th century.

Follow the low lying coastline round Sand Wick and note the White Ayre beach and to the north, the lighthouse on Rova Head. It is a relief to leave the derelict buildings north of Heogan and find activity at Beosetter, where the croft stands by a charming burn with two derelict water mills and other stones by it. The mills were once powered by the Lochs of

Beosetter and the presence of a burnt mound where the burn leaves the loch indicates an ancient settlement site. There is a fine sandy beach. Off Sweyn Ness, the Holm of Gunnista provides a back drop and when you are half way down Aith Voe head up the hill to the most southerly part of the Gunnista settlement. At the road end is a burial ground within a walled enclosure. The foundations of St Ola's church remain and in the north west corner of the enclosure, a fireplace and well have been uncovered. It is the substantial remains of an 18th century mausoleum, however, which dominates the churchyard, but there are no inscriptions, just a small weathered skull and crossbones on the lintel above the entrance. In 1743 Elizabeth Mitchell, the widow of Magnus Henderson, built the mausoleum and buried him there.

Follow a track back down to a pebbly beach on Aith Voe, where salmon cages lie in a sheltered

Circular Walk E: BRESSAY – NORTH CIRCULAR

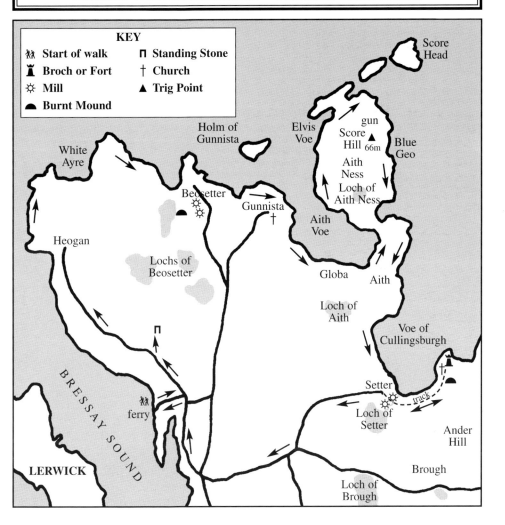

Mausoleum, St Ola's Church, Gunnista, Bressay

position and proceed along the shore. There are large stone enclosures (so much easier to build in Bressay than most parts of Shetland), one of which ends in a small chamber – an otter trap? Helpful stiles take one below Globa to the head of the voe where we head north towards the Loch of Aith Ness. On the west shore there is a ruined haa with massive concrete hard standing and an enclosure to the rear. This was a fish and whale factory which was originally operated by the entrepreneurial Reverend Zachary Hamilton. It eventually closed in 1928.

Behind the ruins of a croft on the hill is a fine cairn. We are now in the major quarrying area of Bressay and much of the stone from Score Hill above Blue Geo had been used for building in Lerwick, including the Town Hall.

Round Elvis Voe (is this a reminder of Celtic Christianity and Elvis, Bishop of Munster who tutored the young St David?) to reach a round-topped hillock at the neck of Aith Ness, thought to have been a broch site. There is no sign of it now, but there is a delightful small

loch separated from the sea by an ayre at Score Minni. You will also spot the islands of Inner and Outer Score, but these are inaccessible.

Climb up to the Trig Point on Score Hill (66m) beside which is the substantial, if rusting, remains of a World War I six-inch naval gun. The gantry used to haul it up from the sea in 1918 also survives. Descend back to the neck of the peninsula at Minni of Aith and choose to either walk the track from Aith croft to Bruntland and then on to Setter, or walk the coast to Setter. At Setter, go through a large metal gate onto a track which goes over the Burn of Setter (two water mill ruins survive) at a bridge incorporating the remains of an old otter trap and out towards the churchyard on the Voe of Cullingsburgh. There is a burnt mound at the end of the track proper and a little further on, adjoining the site of the broch of Cullingsburgh, the churchyard contains the ruins of the 10th century church of St Mary's – the only cross-shaped pre-Reformation chapel in Shetland and until 1727 it was the Parish Church of Bressay. Of note are some ornate gravestones including that commemorating (as translated) "Here lies the brave Commander Claes Jansen Bruyn of Dvrgerdam, died in the service of the Dutch East India Company on 27th August in the year 1636". His ship, the *Amboina*, was returning from Surat, but lost over half her crew from disease. Captain Bruyn died on Bressay and weeks later his ship made it to Texel with her cargo of Persian silk. A table stone grave rests on four square legs and commemorates, "Here lyis in hope of a blessed resurrection the bodie of Margaret ..., a virtuous gentlewoman". (Margaret's surname is now greatly eroded.)

Most famously, the sculptured stone of Cullingsburgh, known as the Bressay Stone, was found here. A replica of the stone will be found in the churchyard, but the original is in the Royal Museum of Scotland in Edinburgh.

It is inscribed with ogham script, one translation of which reads, "The cross of Natdad's daughter, child of Maggddrroann". The "Inventory" thinks the script may have been added later than the scene sculptured on the stone. Under the watchful eye of the derelict Coast Guard watchtower on Ander Hill, make your way back to Setter and the road west which takes one back towards the ferry to Lerwick. The route takes one past Mail Shop, Post Office, Public Hall, and School and next to the Mail Pier, a marina and Bressay Parish Church with its notable 19th century stained glass window and fine wood work.

It can seem a long way back to Maryfield, but the walk is one of Shetland's most memorable and the Maryfield Hotel a very convenient place to revive in.

Front of the Bressay Stone.

Back of the Bressay Stone.

CIRCULAR WALK F ▮▮▮▮▮▮▮▮▮▮

BRESSAY – EAST CIRCULAR
Brough – Ander Hill – Loder Head – Noss Sound – Grutwick – Grimsetter – Brough

8 miles (13 km) : 5 hours

OS Maps: Landranger Sheet 4 Shetland – South Mainland
                Explorer 467 Shetland – Mainland Central
                Explorer 466 Shetland – Mainland South

Panoramic views can be enjoyed on this walk which could include a short visit to Noss. Otherwise take the route to Muckle Hell and the magnificent cliff scenery which follows it.

The small settlement of Brough lies to the north of the road to Noss and after the last house and to its east are the ruins of the broch from which it takes its name and a well preserved burnt mound. The broch has been restored to a large flat-topped mound which rises over 6ft above the bottom of a ditch. A little to its north east is the burnt mound and a

Water pump, CG lookout, Ander Hill, Bressay.

wall which has to be crossed to access the slopes of Ander Hill. Note an array of planticrubs in the area as you climb up to the former Coast Guard lookout. It is now a case of "Childe Roland to the Dark Tower Came" as the floors have been removed and the building is now hollow. A redundant water pump has lost its handle, but still proudly displays its rope and anchor emblem – a reminder of its nautical past. There are splendid views east of Noss to the north, St Mary's Church, Voe of Cullingsburgh and the quarries scarring the slopes of Scora Hill on Aith Ness.

Descend to round Loder Head which boasts a volcanic vent which breaks through the surrounding sandstone and head south to Rules Ness and Geo of Vatsvie. Seals and sea bird activity increases as one approaches the Noss Sound ferry point, an area particularly popular with eider duck. Close to the ferry is a rocky headland with a fine broch ruin about 13ft 6in high. It is thought that considerable remains of original structure still survives beneath the ruin. The banks of earth and stone which also survive indicate that it was a broch of some meaningful size.

There is a tern colony on the shingle beach to be skirted and a keyhole-shaped geo before climbing through a carpet of sea pinks to a cairn. There are good views of Noss and all round the lower slopes of Virdick, off which stands the volcanic vent of Muckle Hell. At Millburn Geo the burn from Loch of Grimsetter once powered a large water mill. Today, the waters of the loch provide a bathing pool for the bonxies.

Broch, Noss Sound, Bressay.

Circular Walk F: BRESSAY – EAST CIRCULAR

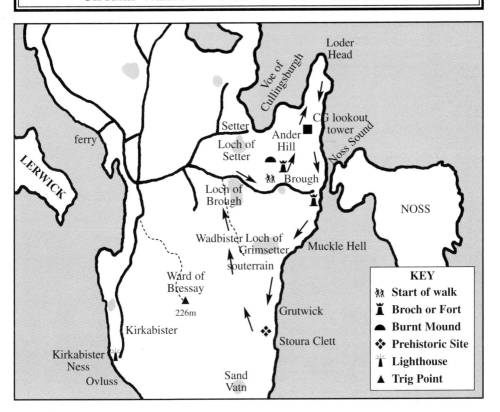

Water mill ruin, Millburn, east coast of Bressay.

Settlement site, east coast of Bressay.

Settlement site, east coast of Bressay.

The cliff scenery is fantastic, but great care is needed as the massive geos bite deep into the cliffs and you need to be quite sure where you are in relation to the cliff edge at all times. Views of the natural arches are best forgotten in windy conditions. Seli Geo is particularly awesome and from here descend to the pebbly beach at Grutwick. A cairn has been created here which commemorates:

> *Erected by the people of Bressay to mark the courageous rescue of the crew of MV Green Lily and the sad loss of William Deacon, winchman of the helicopter. 19-11-97*

Cross a useful bridge over the burn and climb up to Green Head and to a point where one can look down on the Gibraltar-like off-shore stack, Stoura Clett. This stack boasts a triple arch and makes a fitting turn round point for the walk.

Just north of this islet, when Stoura Clett becomes fully visible, climb over the fence and exercise great care to look down on a substantial shelf below. Descend to view two

Memorial at Grutwick, Bressay.

111

Stoura Clett.

dry stone buildings which could have been Celtic monastic cells and then, during the Napoleonic wars, used as a hiding place from the press-gangs.

Return to Grutwick and head round to east side

of the small loch of Seligo. Ascend to an unusual cairn between the deserted crofting area of Wadbister and the cliff edge. Out of sight of the sea, perhaps the cairn warned people of the proximity of the dangerous cliff edge.

Possible monastic site, opposite Stoura Clett.

The crofts at Wadbister have burnt mounds 250yds to the west and 150yds south east further on. An earth house, or souterrain is hidden away behind the ruined croft nearest to the loch. The Wadbister settlement is made up of four crofts close together. Go to the northern wall of the westernmost ruin to find a sharp dip in the ground. At the west end of the almost circular dip, the lintel of the souterrain should be spotted. The dip could be a prehistoric house site with a hearth stove in the middle. The underground chamber was a hiding place and was roughly oval in shape. Maximum length was 6ft 6in and maximum breadth 4ft 6in. The roof was formed of large slabs laid horizontally in an irregular fashion and as the opening was only 2ft high it would be difficult to locate. Thanks to Andy Duffus we found it.

Make for a metal gate in the wall and walk a well-made track past the croft of Gorie to Loch of Brough. This loch is popular with both wildfowl and model yacht enthusiasts and races are a regular feature here.

From the loch, climb up the hill and take a left turn to return to Brough and complete this memorable walk.

Souterrain entrance, Wadbister, Bressay.

Souterrain interior, Wadbister, Bressay.

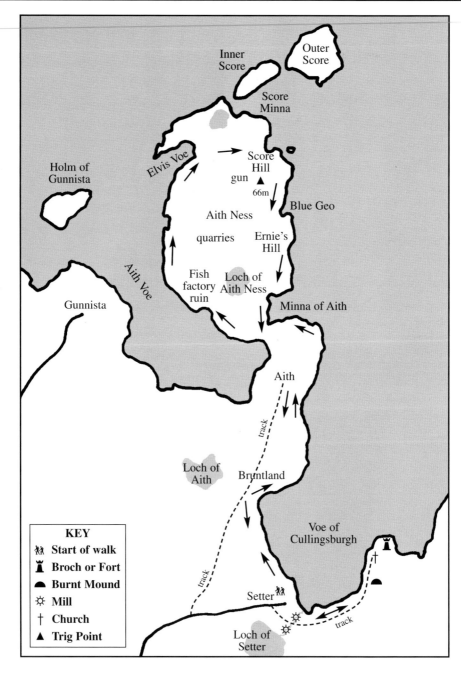

Outer Score

Inner Score

Score Minna

Elvis Voe

Score Hill

gun ▲ 66m

Blue Geo

Holm of Gunnista

Aith Ness

quarries

Ernie's Hill

Fish factory ruin

Loch of Aith Ness

Aith Voe

Gunnista

Minna of Aith

Aith

track

Loch of Aith

Bruntland

Voe of Cullingsburgh

track

KEY
- 🏃 Start of walk
- 🏰 Broch or Fort
- ⛰ Burnt Mound
- ☼ Mill
- † Church
- ▲ Trig Point

Setter 🏃

track

Loch of Setter

CIRCULAR WALK G

BRESSAY – AITH NESS

5 miles (8 km) : 3 hours

OS Maps: Landranger Sheet 4 Shetland – South Mainland
             Explorer 467 Shetland – Mainland Central

A superb walk round Aith Ness, with the opportunity to extend it by visiting the remains of a medieval chapel famous for the Bressay Stone and adjacent broch site. A full description of the area can be found in Walk 5.

The walk starts at Setter which is reached by taking the road towards Noss, leaving it to head north east after Uphouse. From Setter, head up the coastline of Voe of Cullingsburgh or walk the track to Bruntland and on to Aith Croft.

Climb towards Loch of Aith Ness and note on the shore below the ruins of a fish and whale factory which closed in 1928. Round Elvis Voe to reach a round-topped hillock at the neck of

Gun gantry, Score Hill, Aith Ness, Bressay.

Naval gun, Score Hill, Aith Ness, Bressay. Noss and Ander Hill beyond.

Loch and quarries, Aith Ness, Bressay.

Aith Ness, thought to have been a broch site, no sign of it now. There is a delightful small loch separated from the sea by an ayre at Score Minni. The islands of Inner and Outer Score are inaccessible.

Climb up to the Trig Point on Score Hill (66m) beside which is the substantial, if rusting remains of a World War I six-inch naval gun. The gantry used to haul it up from the sea also survives. Descend towards Blue Geo and on Erne's Hill see the remains of the quarrying operations which provided roofing and paving stones for Lerwick.

Descend back to the neck of the peninsula at Minni of Aith and decide whether to walk the track from Aith Croft to Bruntland and on to Setter, or walk the coast to Setter. The look-out on top of Ander Hill is a prominent landmark throughout this walk.

Hopefully you have time to extend the walk from Setter by going through a large metal gate on to a track which goes over the Burn of Setter towards the churchyard on the Voe of Cullingsburgh. There is a burnt mound at the end of the track proper and a little further on, adjoining the site of a broch, is the church site of St Mary's. The churchyard contains some ornamental gravestones and a replica of the sculptured stone of Cullingsburgh, known as the Bressay Stone, which was found in 1864. It is sculptured in relief on the two broad faces. On the front is a cross and two monsters swallowing a small human figure. In the centre is a man on horseback and on each side an ecclesiastic with pointed hood, crosier and book-satchel slung over the shoulder. Below are two beasts. On the back are more beasts and ecclesiastics. There are also two ogham inscriptions which may have been cut later than the carvings.

After exploring the area, make your way back to Setter along the track to complete this walk.

Broch of Cullingburgh, Bressay.

St Mary's Church, Cullingsburgh.

NOSS

5 miles (8 km) : 3 hours

If walking or cycling across Bressay it is 4 miles to Noss Ferry and back, so the total would be 9 miles (15 km), 6 hours

OS Maps: Landranger Sheet 4 Shetland – South Mainland
Explorer 466 Shetland – Mainland South

"If one had to recommend a place where the visitor to Shetland, with limited time and travel facilities could get an impression of the wealth of Shetland's sea bird population – then, it would have to be Noss," so said Shetland's famous naturalist, Bobby Tulloch. The name Noss comes from the Norse for 'a point of rock' and the Noup of Noss, the distinctive highest point of the sheer eastern cliffs, stands 600ft (180m) above the sea and is visible for many miles around. It can be visited from late May to the end of August and you should wait at the sign on the Bressay shore at Noss Sound for a SNH warden to ferry you across in an inflatable dinghy.

Ferryman's Cottage, Bressay.   © **John Reid**

Noss from the Ward of Bressay.

Once ashore, visit the information room in Gungstie – the warden's house. There is also a restored pony pund (1870) which was leased to a County Durham coal mine owner, so that Shetland pony stallions could be bred and supplied as pit-ponies. There are traces of a medieval chapel at Gungstie.

The island is grazed by around 350 Shetland sheep which are brought inside the Hill Dyke during the lambing season and so away from the ground-nesting birds including the great skuas (bonxies). Walk the island anti-clockwise by first visiting the sandy bay of Nesti Voe and move on to a wall with a convenient ladder-stile over it. Climb up above Hellia Cluva and note a small burnt mound. The ascent up Hill of Setter becomes steeper as you round the Point of Hovie to view the Holm of Noss (164ft), a grassy-topped stack once

Circular Walk H: NOSS

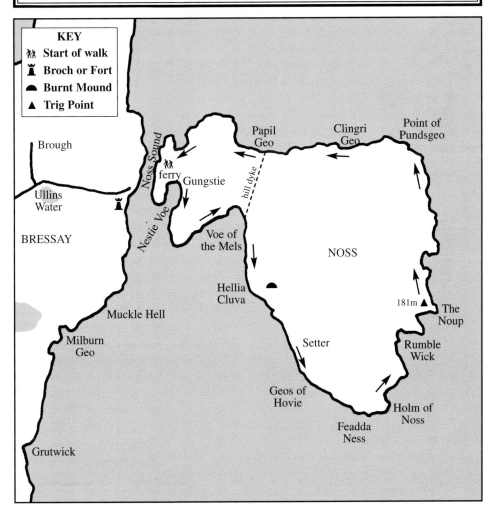

KEY
🏃 Start of walk
🏰 Broch or Fort
🔺 Burnt Mound
▲ Trig Point

Brough

Ullins Water

BRESSAY

Muckle Hell

Milburn Geo

Grutwick

Noss Sound

ferry Gungstie

Nestie Voe

hill dyke

Voe of the Mels

Hellia Cluva

Papil Geo

Clingri Geo

Point of Pundsgeo

NOSS

181m ▲

The Noup

Setter

Rumble Wick

Geos of Hovie

Holm of Noss

Feadda Ness

accessed by the use of a cradle lying on two cables, but mercifully, removed in 1864 when the wall was built along the precipice.

The gannetries on Rumble Wick and on The Noup are white with the guano whence erupts a pungent smell. There are estimated to be 5,500 nests and on the innumerable ledges and niches below are large numbers of guillemots, razorbills, puffins and kittiwakes – all finding food in the fish-rich waters off Noss.

The Trig Point on The Noup (170ft, 181m) is the high point of this walk and from here follow the east coast down past several dramatic geos to North Croo and Papil Geo, where perhaps, Celtic missionaries from Ireland made their land fall in Noss. Cross the Hill Dyke to meet the route back to Gungstie and the ferry to Bressay.

The cradle of Noss. © **John Reid**

CIRCULAR WALK I

COLLAFIRTH

6 miles (10 km) : 5 hours

OS Maps: **Landranger Sheet 2 Shetland – Whalsay**
                  Explorer 468 Shetland – Mainland North East

Collafirth House.

A tough climb up Collafirth Hill to start this walk to a delightful waterfall and a prehistoric settlement site before a gentle return to the start point. Hares and grouse may be spotted.

The road to Collafirth from the A968 north of Voe is not for the faint hearted, particularly in winter but the rewards of visiting this reasonably remote spot are many. At the head of the voe is the Old School House and one can park at the road end near delightfully painted Collafirth House where the burn flows through the garden, under the bridge and into the voe.

Go through the gate at the end of the road and follow the track to the left for about 200 yards. Leave the track entering a field with a stone ruin and make for the left-hand corner. Follow a fence which climbs the hill diagonally north east to the top where the sandy shored Mill Loch should be spotted. Walk round the east side of the loch past a prominent mound to the north east point where the burn leaves the loch and begins its descent to the sea. An arrangement of stones indicates where a sluice gate was fitted to control the flow of water down to a mill, which will be found further down the burn. One hundred yards lower down from the mill is what looks like an abandoned mill construction built into the bank of the burn. From here away to the east, Lunna House and folly can be seen across Swinning Voe. Keep to the left of the burn until after ravine is passed and cross over to descend to near the shore. The splendid waterfall marks the end of

Circular Walk I: COLLAFIRTH

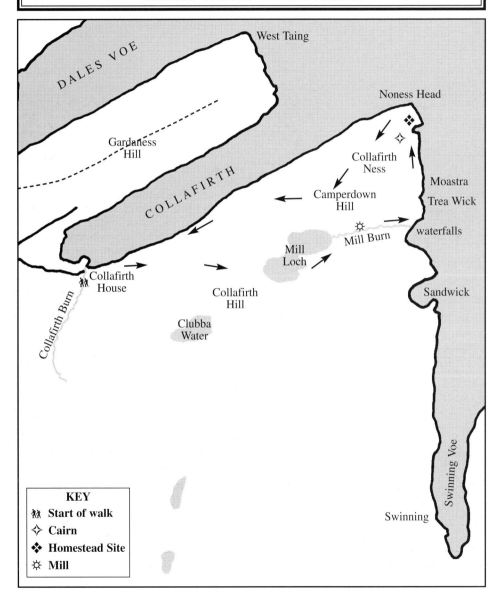

KEY
🏃 **Start of walk**
✧ **Cairn**
❖ **Homestead Site**
☼ **Mill**

Mill Burn waterfall, Swinning Voe, Collafirth Ness.

the journey from Mill Burn and in April it is particularly brilliant with posies of primroses.

Walk north past the banks at Moastra and climb up towards the stone enclosure and prehistoric settlement site on Collafirth Ness. If you look east before the final walk up you may spot a standing stone on a cairn 400 yards up the slope of the hill. This is one of two prehistoric cairns on the ness and has both small upright stones and an upright stone 3ft 3ins high.

From this cairn, head back towards the sea aiming for the stone enclosure on the brow of the hill. The ruined cairn behind the enclosure seems to have been the site of both prehistoric habitation and burial. A cist, built of four large boulders, has a cover slab which is still in place, though tilted. It resembles a miniature cromlech.

From Noness Head aim up the slope of Camperdown Hill (named after the battle in 1797) and descend diagonally down to the shore line of Colla Firth. It is easy going along this sheltered route passing the ruins of a number of crofts as one does so to reach the end of this walk.

Prehistoric settlement site, Noness Head, Collafirth Ness.

CIRCULAR WALK J

OUTRABISTER – POINT OF LUNNA NESS
(Option to include the 'Stones of Stofast')

5 miles (8 km) : 3 hours

OS Maps: **Landranger Sheet 2 Shetland – Whalsay**
                   Explorer 468 Shetland – Mainland North East

A walk in one of the wildest parts of East Mainland, so pick a good day. The house at Outrabister is quite striking in its fresh white paint and will be found right at the end of the unclassified road signposted, initially, to Lunna from the B9071 junction by the shop and community hall at Vidlin. From Lunna continue north east to the road end.

Park in the lay-by at Outrabister and go through a gate to head south east to Neegirth on the opposite coast. At the wire fence, pass through a gate and cross the lush pasture to follow the north shore of Fugla Water with its distinctive islets.

The huge Stones of Stofast dominate the view to the south; high on the hill they resemble the walls of a mighty fortress. It is well worth the

scramble up the hill to explore the 2,000 tonne glacial, erratic boulder split in two by frost.

From Neegirth return to the north shore of Fugla Water where a possible settlement site can be examined, before climbing north on a track between two stone enclosures. On the top of the Ward of Outrabister is a Trig point (90m) and north of it, on the following hill, a solitary stone boulder. Four lochs now lie beneath one with Mill Loch on the east shore the largest.

Aim for West Loch and keep inland from Stour Hevda and Wick of Glachon. The Hill of State (spot height 59m) is the objective and it is quite steep in parts. Descend to follow the valley north. On a tongue of land in the next valley is the ruin of a small house (a welcome

Stones of Stofast

124

sight)! Descend the hill towards the coastline and a sheep fold enclosure. We now lose the views of Whalsay and Skerries, but gain those looking north, including Fetlar and Saxa Vord on Unst.

From the Point of Lunna Ness the island of Lunna Holm seems very near; pass a small shingle beach and walk Scora Dale to Feor Wick. Just before Riven Noust is a mill ruin beside the burn coming down from Mill Loch.

Go through a metal gate and pass a shingle beach and a stone wall at the end of a fence. The Trig Point on Ward of Outrabister is clearly visible south east, whilst to the north, the houses of Burravoe, Yell, particularly the Old Haa and Overby, can be spotted as well as the Stack of the Horse. Walk through lush pasture to arrive back at Outrabister and enjoy looking at a large selection of collectables on sale in Frank Watt's outbuildings.

Circular Walk J: OUTRABISTER – POINT OF LUNNA NESS

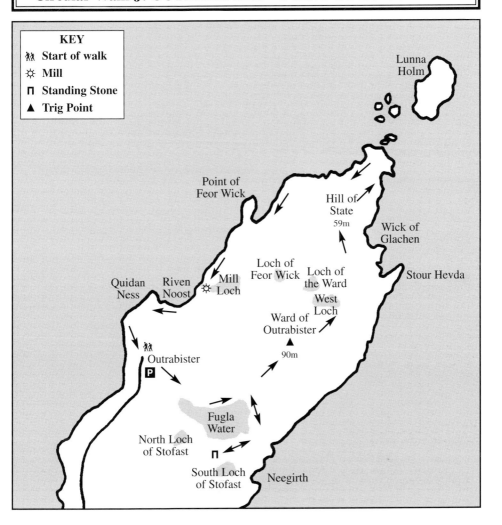

KEY
- 👫 **Start of walk**
- ☼ **Mill**
- ⊓ **Standing Stone**
- ▲ **Trig Point**

CIRCULAR WALK K ████████████████████████

LUNNING HEAD
Lunning – Lunning Head – Orra Wick

5 miles (8 km) : 3 hours

OS Maps: Landranger Sheet 2 Shetland – Whalsay
Explorer 468 Shetland – Mainland North East

A fine standing stone, prehistoric homestead site and excellent views from Lunning Head combine to make this an excellent stroll. One small climb up to the Trig Point at Lunning Head.

The drive or cycle to Lunning takes one from Vidlin on a winding route for about three miles. Pass Loch of Gerda Water, Longa Water and Gollins Water before arriving at the small and ancient settlement of Lunning. To its south, the burn coming down from Mill Loch once powered two water mills. Parking can be a problem as there is little space.

From the road end, climb over the fence to see the standing stone on the east side of the road.

It is of irregular shape rising to a height of 6ft. Descend the slope to the coastline and the Skerry of Lunning, popular with seals, before heading over The Knowes of Ramna Geo. Aim north west up the slope to find a prehistoric homestead site on a shelf below, which is easily identifiable but can get covered in bracken. It is well preserved, standing up to 3ft (1m) high and about 30ft (10m) in diameter. The thick wall surrounding the interior has traces of four alcoves. The entrance was on the south side.

Continue the climb past a distinctive white, quartz rock to reach the Trig Point (65m) on top of Lunning Head. There are magnificent and extensive views from here and both the

Planticrub, Lunning. Whalsay beyond.

folly and church of Lunna can be seen way to the west.

Walk down to Mossie Geo, passing a distinctive boulder and on to the rocky beach at Orra Wick with its now redundant winch.

From here either return the way you came or head due south across open country to return to the road end at Lunning.

Homestead site, Lunning Head.

Circular Walk K: LUNNING HEAD

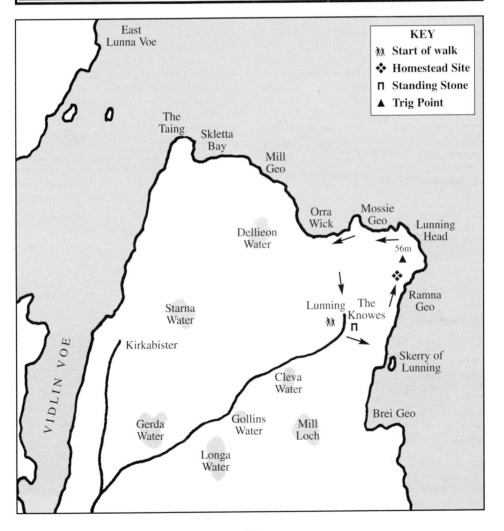

CIRCULAR WALK L

BRETTABISTER
Brettabister – Hill of Neap

5 miles (8 km) : 4 hours

OS Maps: **Landranger Sheet 2 Shetland – Whalsay**
                    Explorer 467 Shetland – Mainland Central

A walk along a fine stretch of coastline on easy terrain with a small climb round Hill of Neap. A broch site, prehistoric fort, mills and burnt mounds all add to the interest of this enjoyable stroll.

Park near the red granite and marble monument in memory of the men of North Nesting who gave their lives in the two World Wars. It is in a prominent site above the junction at Brettabister for the road to Laxo and Housabister. Walk north east down the road towards Housabister and at the Church of Scotland church, visit the small memorial area for former ministers. The most poignant memorial tells of a minister's family, all of whom predeceased him. Behind the church is the remains of a broch which originally measured about 220ft in circumference at the outer wall. An enormous number of stones were used in its construction and the church is almost wholly built from stones from the broch. The broch was in a good position being near the top of the cliffs and virtually unapproachable from the sea. Continue down the road past Housabister; to the north a burn

Broch, Housabister. Hill of Neap beyond.

flows down from Loch of Kirkabister beside which are the remains of a burnt mound. Walk through Kirkabister past a burial ground and medieval chapel site (dedicated to St Olaf) and leave the road to follow the coastline from Wick of Kirkabister. The cliffs are often sheer between here and Ura Stack. Climb the Hill of Neap on which there are two cairn stones, but neither are positioned at the highest part of it. (Spot height 47m).

As you walk down the northern slopes enjoy excellent views of Hog Island with its natural arch and adjacent Stang Hog. There is no access to Hog Island but on the landward side

of the narrow channel, between the coastline and the island, are three rampart remains of an iron-age promontory fort which has been cut off by the sea.

From Wick of Neap with its two noosts, follow a fence up to a derelict croft house where a track heads south to a gate and the road-end is reached below the prominent house at Neap.

Walk the road back to Brettabister enjoying sights of a duck pond, rockery gardens and ruined water mills once powered by Burn of the Waters that bubble down the hill opposite the church.

Circular Walk L: BRETTABISTER

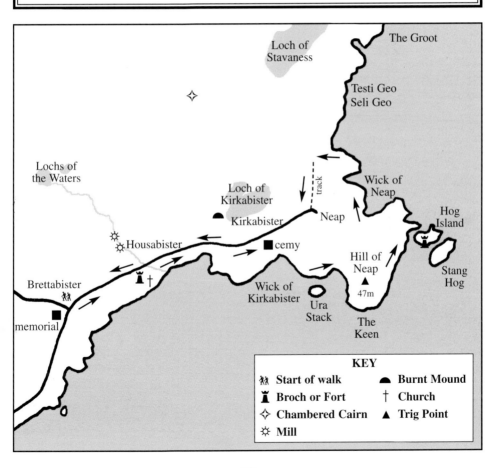

KEY

🏃 **Start of walk**   🔺 **Burnt Mound**
🏰 **Broch or Fort**   † **Church**
✧ **Chambered Cairn**   ▲ **Trig Point**
☼ **Mill**

Site of Iron Age fort, Hill of Neap. Hog Island and Whalsay beyond.

Natural arch, Hog Island.

CIRCULAR WALK M

ESWICK (SOUTH NESTING)

3 miles (5 km) : 4 hours

OS Maps: Landranger Sheet 3 Shetland – North Mainland
Explorer 467 Shetland – Mainland Central

A great stroll round the Moul of Eswick which includes the cliffs where a lighthouse was destroyed and an unusual garden seat.

From the B9075 road in South Nesting follow the unclassified road east to Skellister, Brough and the road end at Eswick.

A track to the lighthouse via Muckle Loch heads east from the Eswick croft; do not take it unless wishing to shorten the walk. Head south to South Bay of Eswick and from here climb up the slopes of Ward of Eswick and find a possible refreshment spot and a garden seat which sits stoically high on the cliffs – great view, but it can be breezy and care is needed as ever on the cliffs. Climb up round The Flaach below which is Fru Stack. The lighthouse is comparatively new and was constructed here when its predecessor went over the cliffs some years ago. To the south, offshore, the light on Hoo Stack may be spotted. There is another to

Cliffs like old gnarled faces. Moul of Eswick.

the north east on Inner Voder. Hevda Skerry is popular with singing seals.

Croo Geo boasts a cave which resembles a natural arch and from here climb round the headland into Es Wick. The views include Whalsay, Skerries, Bressay, Ling Ness and South Nesting Bay. Descend to cross a burn, pass a loose arrangement of stones and follow an ancient cart track to connect with the road end at Eswick. If time allows admire the plantation of mixed trees created by Terry Rodgers and enjoy a swim on the beach at Es Wick.

Circular Walk M: ESWICK (SOUTH NESTING)

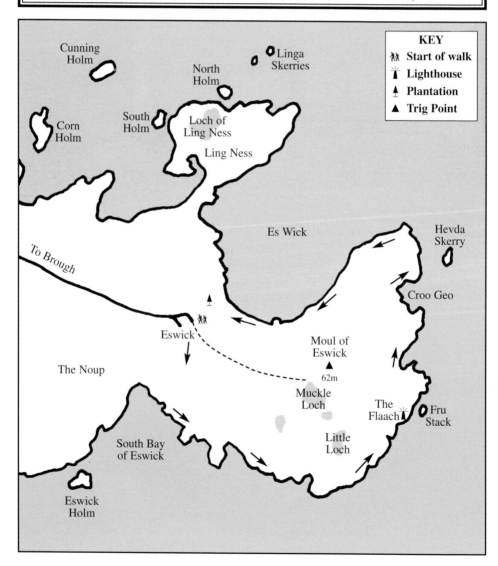

Lighthouse, The Flaach, Moul of Eswick.

GLETNESS

2 miles (3 km) : 2 hours

OS Maps: **Landranger Sheet 3 Shetland – North Mainland
Explorer 467 Shetland – Mainland Central**

This short walk takes one along Glet Ness, a popular haven with otters and sea birds. Enjoy an excellent sight of the Isles on easy terrain, apart from a slightly rocky section on the Ness.

John T Barclay wrote the words and music for his beautiful song 'Da Isles o Gletness' expressing his love for them however far away he may be:

> *"Tho I go rovin fae hame at A'm lovin,
> Bidin afar wi da idder exiles,
> What ever da pairt be, here will my
>   hert be,
> Linkit for ever ta hame an da isles."*

At the road end at Gletness, reached on an unclassified road from the B9075 near Catfirth, South Nesting, park near a small house. Head for the shore, by using three stiles, to arrive at a pebble beach. Offshore the North and South Isles of Gletness, Stunger and Tainga Skerry are just some of the eye-catching attractions with the lighthouse on Hoo Skerry and South Skerry also visible. Shetland ponies may also be about. Follow the rocky foreshore past Hawks Ness and head out on the southern side of the ness. It is a popular place for otters but even if they are as elusive as ever, there is plenty of bird life to enjoy. Half way down the ness is a rocky section which is

Gletness, Nesting.

easily surmountable and at the point of the ness is a sheltered spot for a break.

Return on the north side with its great views of North Voe of Gletness and join the track coming down from North House to the main road.

One can now return either along the shore or walk the unclassified road back to its end at Gletness. Hopefully, it will be a case of, "Peerie waves dancin, sunsheen a – glansin, Bringing ta brichtness da grey o da sea," to enhance your memories of this notable walk.

Circular Walk N: GLETNESS

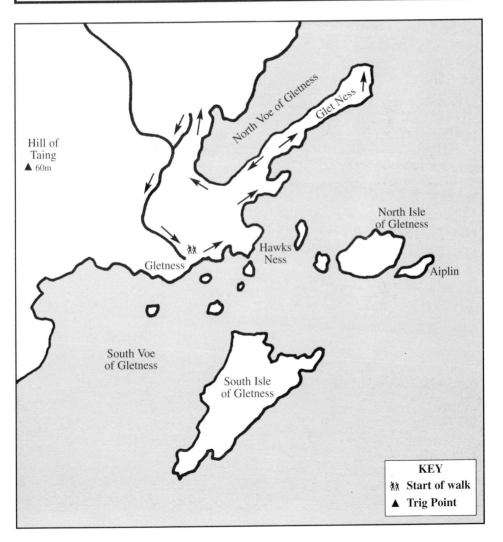

Hill of Taing
▲ 60m

North Voe of Gletness

Glet Ness

North Isle of Gletness

Hawks Ness

Gletness

Aiplin

South Voe of Gletness

South Isle of Gletness

KEY
🚶🚶 **Start of walk**
▲ **Trig Point**

North Isle of Gletness, Nesting.

CIRCULAR WALK O

WADBISTER NESS

5 miles (8 km) : 3 hours

OS Maps: Landranger Sheet 3 Shetland – North Mainland
Explorer 467 Shetland – Mainland Central

A walk round Wadbister Ness with its fine cliff scenery, a broch site and open views from Lambgarth Head.

From Gott take the unclassified road to Laxfirth to leave it where it forms a junction with the long track to North Hamarsland.

Walk the well surfaced track, enjoying views of Lax Firth and cross the Burn of North Hamarsland and reach the extensive property set in an enviable position. From here bear north east to the shore at Otter Point passing a stone cairn; by the pebbly beach on the Ayre of Breiwick is a circular stone ruin.

Go round Lambgarth Head and after Mitten, reach the Point of Wadbister Ness. The broch (not OS marked) of this ness will be found a little way into Wadbister Voe on about the third rocky spur which juts out into the voe. Difficult to access because of the jagged rock formation, most of this broch has been swept away by the sea, but enough remains to identify it.

Make your way south west along peat banks to reach a stone enclosure and wire fence. Cross a footbridge and reach the planticrubs which herald approaching dwellings. There is a splendidly restored stone building by a pebble

Broch, Wadbister Ness.

beach with its own noost and winch. Ascend to and cross the field which lies between the shore and Wadbister House where trees flourish at the road end. Walk the road passing more houses built along the shore and a salmon farm service area until Black Loch is reached.

Head south from the road to follow the east shore of Black Loch and reach the unclassified road to Laxfirth near Loch of Vatster.

Follow the road back to the start point near South Hamarsland to complete this walk.

Circular Walk O: WADBISTER NESS

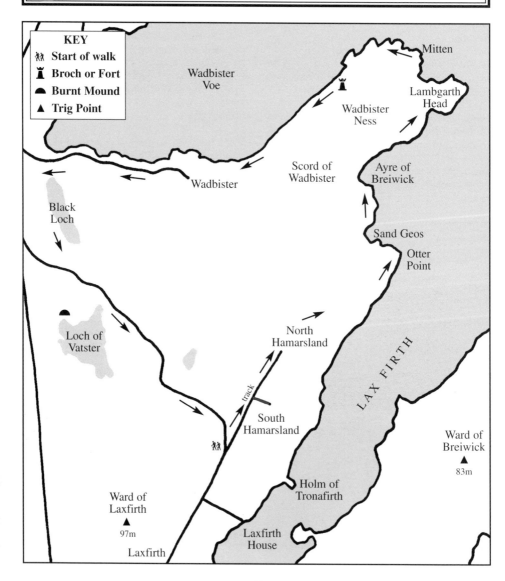

KEY
- 𝕩𝕩 **Start of walk**
- 𝕚 **Broch or Fort**
- ◣ **Burnt Mound**
- ▲ **Trig Point**

Wadbister Voe

Mitten

Wadbister Ness

Lambgarth Head

Scord of Wadbister

Ayre of Breiwick

Wadbister

Black Loch

Sand Geos

Otter Point

Loch of Vatster

North Hamarsland

South Hamarsland

LAX FIRTH

Ward of Breiwick
▲
83m

track

Ward of Laxfirth
▲
97m

Laxfirth

Holm of Tronafirth

Laxfirth House

CIRCULAR WALK P

HAWKS NESS

4 miles (6 km) : 3 hours

OS Maps: **Landranger Sheet 3 Shetland – North Mainland**
Explorer 467 Shetland – Mainland Central

There is so much to enjoy on this walk round Hawks Ness, that plenty of time has been allowed for it. Excellent coastal scenery, particularly on Brim Ness and a fine broch site on the headland. A short cross country section to complete this walk over Ward of Breiwick. (83m)

From Gott take the unclassified road to North Califf and then head north to Breiwick and the road end. Commence the walk here.

Breiwick has a wide shingle bay with several houses. After the last house, head straight on to reach Foraness Voe which is an area of great beauty. There is a small natural arch on the east side of the bay and distant views include Kebister and Ander Hill on Bressay. A croft ruin will be found on the shoulder of the hill at Houbies, the last we shall find for a while. Brim Ness has a large cave and on the Bight of Brimness is a notable natural arch going three ways. The sheets of metal on the beach are from a barge wrecked on the rocks in the 1980s.

We are now approaching the point of Hawks Ness where a dry stone wall runs down to a small sheep pund. The stones in the wall would have come from the broch which stood on the

Natural arch, Fora Ness.

high rocky knoll close to the edge of the cliff fence. Overall diameter is about 55ft and there appears to have been a narrow opening in the wall towards the north east. This is a great place to sit and enjoy a break and the view of South Nesting to the north.

Between Hawks Ness and South Isle of Gletness is the Unicorn Rock named after the *Unicorn* which sank on the rock on 25th August, 1567.

Follow the coast line round into Lax Firth leaving it to climb east from the distinctive Skerby Ayre which is made up of pebbles and home to a tern colony. Climb over Ward of Breiwick (83m) and head down to Breiwick, past North House, to complete this walk.

Circular Walk P: HAWKS NESS

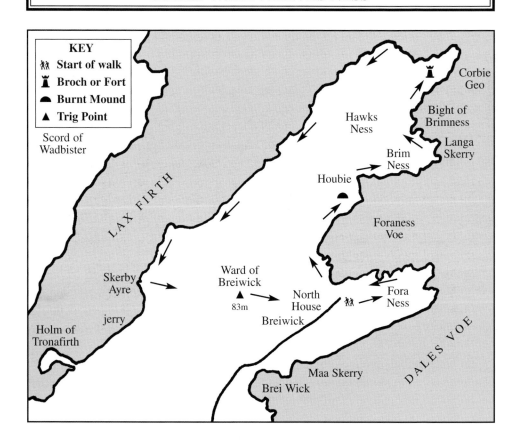

KEY
🚶 Start of walk
♟ Broch or Fort
🔺 Burnt Mound
▲ Trig Point

Scord of Wadbister

LAX FIRTH

Hawks Ness

Corbie Geo

Bight of Brimness

Langa Skerry

Brim Ness

Houbie

Foraness Voe

Skerby Ayre

Ward of Breiwick
▲
83m

North House

Fora Ness

jerry

Breiwick

Holm of Tronafirth

DALES VOE

Maa Skerry

Brei Wick

Queen Street Methodist Mission, Huddersfield, Rambling Group, 1950. A suitably serious author with staff and muddy knees (right). Outdoor clothing had yet to reach the sophistication found today!

© Gwithian Guy

ACKNOWLEDGEMENTS

I am indebted to the authors and editors of the following books and magazine articles and people who have helped me:

The Medieval churches and chapels of Shetland	R. G. Cant	1975
Shetland's Northern Links	Ed. Doreen J. Waugh	1996
Songs and Sights of Shetland	Christine M. Guy	1995
Shetland Shipwrecks	Shetland Sub-Aqua Club	1989
A Guide to Prehistoric Shetland	Noel Fojut	1981
A Guide to Prehistoric and Viking Shetland	Noel Fojut	1994
A Guide to Shetland's Breeding Birds	Bobby Tulloch	1992
A Description of the Shetland Islands	Samuel Hibbert	1822
Shetland	Robert Cowie	1874
Guide to Shetland	Dr Mortimer Manson	1942
The Orkneys and Shetland	John R. Tudor	1883
A Brief Description of Orkney and Zetland	John Brand	1701
A Tour through the Islands of Orkney and Shetland	George Low	1774
Reminiscences of a Voyage to Shetland	Christian Ployen	1896
Art Rambles in Shetland	John Reid	1869
Shetland III ('The Inventory') The Ancient and Historic Monuments of Scotland	Royal Commission	1946
Shetland Life Magazine	Editor James R. Nicolson	
Pochin Memorial	Michael Lowe	1990
Shetland Field Study Walks	Jill Slee Blackadder	1998
Shetland	Jill Slee Blackadder	2003
The Chambered Tombs of Scotland vols 1 & 2	Audrey Shore Henshall	1965
Burnt Mound papers (including extracts from National Monuments record of Scotland up to 1989)	John Cruse	
Iron Age Promontory Forts in the Northern Isles BAR British Series 79	Raymond Lamb	1980
Shetland — An illustrated architectural guide	Mike Finnie	1990
The Life of Sir Walter Scott	J. G. Lockhart	1896
Coastal Settlements of the North, Scottish Archaeological Forum Vol. 5	Raymond Lamb	1973
Lerwick Town Hall — A Guide	Dr Mortimer Manson	
Offshore – A North Sea Journey	A. Alvarez	1986
The Saga of a Ship, The Earl of Zetland	Adam Robson	1982
Airfield Focus No 13, Sullom Voe and Scatsta	Peter Ward	1994
A Walk in Shetland by Two Eccentrics	Anon	1831
Prehistoric Rock Art	Stan Beckinsall & Tim Laurie	1998
A History of Scatsta Airfield	Terry Mayes	2001
Cloud Cover	Derek Gilpin Barnes	1943
The Sea Kingdoms	Alistair Moffat	2001
Bressay	Jonathan Wills	1990
South East Bressay Walk	Laurence F. Anderson	2000
Arctic Airmen	Ernest Schofield & Roy Conyers Nesbit	1987

ACKNOWLEDGEMENTS

The Royal Commission on the Ancient and Historic Monuments of Scotland for the illustrations: Fugla Ness Broch; Stoura Clett Structures; Whalsay, Loch of Huxter Fort; Whalsay, Brough Cup-Markings; © RCAHMS Acknowledgement to: The Society of Antiquaries of Scotland, Bressay Cullingsburgh Cross Slab, Ogham-Inscribed (SH 1395), Bressay, Cullingsburgh Cross Slab, Ogam- Inscribed (SH14); © RCAHMS Acknowledgement to: The Society of Antiquaries of Scotland, Lunnasting Stone; © RCAHMS Inventory of The Ancient Monuments of Orkney and Shetland, vol III, 1946, p.63, Lerwick, Fort Charlotte; Crown Copyright: Royal Commission on the Ancient and Historic Monuments of Scotland.

I would like to acknowledge the work of the RCHAMS field workers for their contributions to the inventories of Shetland which started in the late 1920s and finished in 1937, but were not published until 1946 due to the war. The field investigators were mainly, Mr John Corrie, Mr C. S. T. Calder (who did most of the drawings), Mr G. P. H. Watson and at the very end, Mr Angus Graham. I was helped considerably by Kristina Johansson, NMRS Public Orders, for this information and assistance with images.

Thanks to Harper Collins Publishers for permission to reproduce the poem, "Pangur Ban" published in 2002 in the book, "The Sea Kingdoms", © author, Alistair Moffat. (ISBN 0 00 653243 8) Copyright in the customised version vests in Shetland Times Ltd.

Other photographs as follows:
Spitfire wall painting, Old Kirk, Scatsta; Terry Mayes. The Morrison family at Sandwick, by Bobby Tulloch with the kind permission of Mary Ellen Odie. Pochin's Monument, Girlsta Loch; Courtesy of Shetland Museum Photographic Archive, © Shetland Museum. Bressay, the Giant's Leg; Edward Foster; Courtesy of Shetland Museum Photographic Archive, © Shetland Museum. Queen St. Methodist Mission Rambling Group, Huddersfield, Gwithian Guy. All other photographs taken by Peter Guy or Catherine Ginger.

Songs:
'Da Isles o Gletness'; John T Barclay and 'Da Sealkie Wife's Sang'; Mary Ellen Odie are published in the book, 'Songs and Sights of Shetland', compiled by Christine M. Guy published by Shetland Arts Trust in association with the Education Department of Shetland Islands Council © 1995 Shetland Arts Trust. Both songs were sung and recorded by The Yell Lasses Choir on their cassette tape, 'A Sight of the Isles'. (Viking Vision ZE 025). Words for the Sullom Voe Song; Reg Curwen (ex 210 Flying Boat Squadron).

Thanks to Shetland Library and to the Shetland Museums Service and the following people who assisted me in various ways: Robbie Simpson, David Cooper, Andy and Jenny Bradley, John and Wendy Scott, Andy Duffus, Gordon and Marjorie Williamson, Jamie Jamieson, Terry Mayes, Charlie Laurenson, Donny Mackay, Mavis Tait, Mary Ellen Odie, Willie Hughson.

All publications in this series owe their existence to the "Around the Isles" articles by "Hundiclock" published in "Sullom Voe Scene" and reporting by Nigel Martin. Grateful thanks to Catherine Ginger who prepared the book for publication.

Advice on accommodation is given by the Tourist Information Centre, Shetland Islands Tourism, Market Cross, Lerwick, Shetland ZE1 OLU. Telephone: 01595 693434.